DATE DUE

NO 16 '92			
JY 2 '93			
JY 16 '93			
JY 30 '93			
MY 2 '99			
AG 9 01			
FE 12 09			

DEMCO 38-296

Also by Steven Carter and Julia Sokol

MEN WHO CAN'T LOVE
WHAT SMART WOMEN KNOW
WHAT REALLY HAPPENS IN BED

LIVES
WITHOUT
BALANCE

LIVES
WITHOUT
BALANCE

WHEN YOU'RE GIVING
EVERYTHING YOU'VE GOT
AND STILL NOT GETTING
WHAT YOU HOPED FOR

Steven Carter
and
Julia Sokol

VILLARD BOOKS ■ New York ■ 1992

Library of Congress Cataloging-in-Publication Data
Carter, Steven
Lives without balance: when you're giving everything
you've got and still not getting what you hoped for
Steven Carter and Julia Sokol.—1st ed.
p.   cm.
ISBN 0-394-58814-2
1. Conduct of life.   2. Disappointment.   3. Success.   I. Title.
BF637.C5C36   1992   158—dc20   91-58012

Designed by: Carla Weise/Levavi & Levavi
Manufactured in the United States of America
9 8 7 6 5 4 3 2
First edition

FOR THE CREATURES WHO HELPED US MAINTAIN
A SENSE OF BALANCE:

Carla, Maggie, Paddington, and Tulip

Acknowledgments

We would like to thank all the people who have helped us, but special thanks must first go to Peter Coopersmith who convinced us of the need for this book and whose creative contribution has been invaluable. We are most grateful to the interviewees who gave so generously of themselves so that others might benefit from hearing their stories. We also want to acknowledge our editor Diane Reverand for being so supportive of the concept. A special word of appreciation must go to Lloyd Sheldon Johnson, Alan Suchman, Norman Haggie, Cheryl Pelavin, Bob Tabian, M. J. Kelly, Ken Starr, Adam Robinson, Stacey Cahn, Nancy Brandeis, and Violet Woodhouse, C.F.P. Last, but far from least, our thanks go to Don Schimelfenig for his patience, support, and flexibility.

Contents

Introduction

◄

FOR MANY OF US, IT FEELS AS IF IT HAPPENED OVERNIGHT. There we were, working hard, cruising along on our chosen paths, sure we had made the right choices and excited about our prospects for the future. Then, suddenly, nothing was working the way we anticipated. No matter how hard we worked, no matter how much we gave, we weren't getting what we hoped for, and we couldn't understand what went wrong.

If the life you are living right now is not the life you had in mind, you are not alone. Millions of people, just like you, are taking a long hard look at their lives—at the promises and the realities—and wondering what happened. They want to know how to make their lives more tolerable, and they want to make sure they don't repeat the mistakes that got them stuck in the first place. If this sounds like you, this book is written to help you get a better life.

Not the "Rich and Famous" kind of "better" life—complete with resort-size swimming pools, chauffeur-driven limousines, and closets full of snakeskin boots—unless that wouldn't add to your already burdensome credit card debt. Nor the *Town and Country* kind of life with horses grazing in your backyard and 250 of your nearest and dearest joining you for lunch under the tent—unless paying for all those oats and all that watercress wouldn't increase the number of hours you or your spouse would have to work each week.

We don't even mean the kind of life Donald Trump used to have—with a yacht too large to sail by oneself, houses too enormous to decorate by oneself, and debts too overwhelming to manage even with the help of half the banks in New York City. And we certainly don't mean the "good life" of an upscale New York attorney—with mortgage payments that are higher than most normal salaries and blood pressure readings to match.

So what kind of better life are we talking about? A better life to us means having a life you can enjoy here and now, today, tomorrow or next Thursday—not next year, five years from now, or when you retire. It means not letting your great ambitions overshadow your small daily successes. It means being comfortable in the present and less obsessed with the future.

The more people we talk to, the clearer it becomes that few of us are enjoying that kind of life. Instead we've become like a nation of mountain climbers, all out of breath, scrambling over rocky and dangerous terrain, each hoping to reach a plateau where there will be some form of payoff for our efforts. Most of us want to make enough money to pay for the climb; many of us want to appreciate the view and feel a sense of accomplishment that can't be taken away; others will be satisfied with no more than a few free, unstressed, minutes for lunch. It appears as though everywhere we go, a disproportionate number of hardworking men and women are complaining that no matter how hard they try, they are not receiving these well-deserved rewards.

In short, for many of us something has gone terribly wrong. We work too much, owe too much, and worry too much. We are enmeshed in life-styles that are giving us far too little for too much effort. Consequently, we're always playing catch-up and are never where we want to be; everyone's struggling, and everyone's stressed.

Why has this happened? Some might say that it's long-overdue punishment for a self-indulgent decade of "yuppie greed." But we don't see it that way. Sure, we have all read about Ivan Boesky's greed and Michael Milken's five-hundred-million-dollar-a-year salary, but what does that have to do with the real world? How many of us have caught so much as a fleeting glimpse of that kind of life?

Yes, there was a period of a few years during which the business pages inundated us with advice telling us to buy real estate, and yes, some men and women were able to buy co-ops and houses. But now these same people are leveraged to the hilt and drowning in mortgage and maintenance costs, and others are still berating themselves because they were unable to get into the real estate market.

Yes, some of us put on exercise gear and joined health clubs, but that one hour a day may be the only positive thing we are doing for ourselves. Yes, some of us renovated eighty-year-old houses and gentrified one-hundred-year-old neighborhoods, but that doesn't change the economic realities for two-career couples struggling with child care and barely able to afford a fifteen-year-old babysitter. Yes, some of us have indulged in more conspicuous consumption than we care to remember, but our monthly credit card payments will continue to keep those memories alive long after our purchases have worn out.

The facts are these: We crafted our futures based upon certain understandings and assumptions that have proved to be incorrect. Too many of us worry that we will never be able to buy a house and too many others worry that we will lose the equity on the ones we already own. Most of us are working longer hours, getting less in terms of real dollars, and suffering from more stress-related symptomatology than our doctors can bear.

Obviously we cannot force solutions from situations over which we have no control; it goes without saying that we cannot single-handedly change government policies and dynamics, redirect powerful social forces, or alter human nature. But many of the problems that are currently affecting each of our lives are the direct result of our own personal policies and dynamics, our own social circumstances, and our own human nature.

These are the factors that have brought us to certain choices and created the behavior patterns and scenarios that are uniquely our own. Even though we cannot change the past, nor can we individually change the world, each of us can take certain steps to change our own way of being, hence restructuring our futures.

That's what this book is all about: changing your pattern and changing your life scenario so that you re-create your identity and write your own definitions of success.

We firmly believe that your current life-style doesn't have to be a life sentence.

I

CHASING THE PROMISE

Fifteen years ago, if someone had told me that I would be having this kind of struggle, I wouldn't have believed him. Now every day I tell myself that just because I have a good practice doesn't mean that I can have all the things that the American dream told me I could have. I've worked very hard to get where I am, but for me the promises haven't come true. I have a terrific education. I have a solid profession. It's logical that I started out with high expectations. People told me that I would be able to do anything I wanted, and I guess I could—if I didn't want to do very much.

—FORTY-YEAR-OLD DENTIST

1

High Expectations and Elusive Payoffs

■◤

IF YOU FEEL FRUSTRATED WITH YOUR GOALS, DISAPPOINTED in your life-style, disillusioned by your dreams, scared of your reality, and exhausted from your work load, you are not alone. All across America, men and women are pulling themselves out of bed in the morning, staring at their bleary-eyed reflections in the mirror, questioning their life choices, and asking, "What happened?" From the executive on the top floors of San Francisco's TransAmerica Building to the computer operator on the graveyard shift in New York's World Trade Center; from the doctor in the emergency room of Boston's Mass. General to the trainee in the Los Angeles mail room of the William Morris Agency—many of us are exhausted from trying to "make it" and worn out from the life-style sacrifices we are enduring while pursuing the money and/or success payoff.

When we talk to people about this, typically they say they feel as though they're giving everything they've got, and they're still not getting what they hoped for. No matter how hard they work, no matter how many hours they put in, no matter how much energy and thought they expend, they feel stuck in lives that seem to be askew or lopsided. They never seem to be able to reach that magical place where they will be able to relax, reap the benefits of hard work, and begin to enjoy their lives. They have lost their center and with it their sense of balance.

These people tell us they are worried about their futures and haunted by debts from their past. They say they put too much emphasis on their careers and now they are distressed by what they perceive to be a profound sense of imbalance in their lives. They don't know how to go about changing accordingly. They say they started out with high expectations for a secure future, adequate leisure time, and a comfortable life-style, but their hopes are not being fulfilled. Their American dream is failing them. Consequently, not only do they feel frustrated and exhausted, they feel as though their anxieties are enmeshing them in life-styles that are all work and worry.

These are not malcontents or nonachievers. These are smart and savvy men and women who pursued what appeared to be solid career tracks. They have good educations; they are dressed for success; they are prepared to work long hours. By any standards, they would be described as goal oriented and success driven. In short, these are men and women who tried to maximize their potential by doing everything they were told would give them an edge.

But instead of achieving their high expectations, these people say that their returns are marginal. No matter what their goals, whether they are concerned primarily with money, personal satisfaction, leisure time, or building a secure future, they feel as though they are struggling for an elusive payoff that always seems within their grasp, but never quite materializes. In short, they feel as though they are often giving everything they've got and getting far less than they expect or deserve. Consider the stories of the men and women that follow. Their situations illustrate the kinds of struggles so many of us are experiencing at this very moment:

Beth is a thirty-three-year-old advertising exec. She has a fancy title, a nice office, a sixty-hour-a-week work schedule, no social life, an undersized studio apartment, and more expenses than she can afford on her salary. She's frustrated because she lives with the feeling that, no matter how diligently she works, her job could disappear tomorrow, and she doesn't see how she will ever be able to afford to live a comfortable, balanced life.

◄

Daniel, twenty-seven, is overwhelmingly depressed because of the employment situation he faced when he got out of college. Despite his Ivy League education, he is still living at home and working as a poorly paid assistant at a film company, where he is constantly reminded that he is fortunate even to have a job.

◄

Janice and Ken, both in their late thirties, are distraught and anxious because Janice recently lost her job and Ken's promotions and salary increases have not kept up with inflation. They don't know how much longer they will be able to pay the mortgage on the apartment they bought in 1986 when prices were going through the roof. Recently they put their apartment on the market, but they have been told that, even if they do find a buyer, it is unlikely that they will be able to sell it for as much as they paid for it.

◄

Ned, fifty, is the proprietor of a men's clothing store that his grandfather started in 1925. Four years ago, his already-solid business was booming, and he behaved accordingly by enlarging into the space next door. Meanwhile, the neighborhood started to change, and his business could not compete with the new malls that were going up all over. Right now, his overhead is huge and he is facing the possibility of being forced to close down a business that has been the mainstay of his entire family. He feels overwhelmed by a sense of futility and defeat.

◄

Alex is in a complete panic. He has been out of work for seven months, something he could never imagine happening to someone who has been so careful about his life plan. He has an MBA from the "best" school along with an impressive undergraduate degree. Only a few years ago, Alex was on his way up and so were his friends, some of whom were making bonuses larger than most people's salaries. He is deeply embar-

rassed by the fact that he has to collect unemployment. As terrifying as staying unemployed is, he is just as frightened at the prospect of ever again working under the kind of pressure he experienced in corporate America.

◄

Meg, thirty-nine, is a doctor with a practice that anyone would consider successful. With the cost of malpractice insurance, office help, rent, and utilities, she feels that she is struggling harder than she did when she first left school. On top of that, child care is expensive and unreliable. She would like to take more time off to spend at home with her four-year-old daughter and eighteen-month-old son, but she doesn't see how she can do it. Surely she has worked hard enough and paid enough dues to get more pleasure out of her life.

The question is, *What happened?* And who is to blame? Is it the fault of the system? Or did each of us independently create our own personal set of frustrations and disappointments? The fact is that when we stop to think about it, we realize that the blame is twofold. Yes, the "system" conspired to serve up faulty expectations, something we'll discuss later in this book, but blame cannot fall entirely on the system. Let's admit it, we are also at fault. To some extent or another, each of us has actively participated in this "conspiracy" by making choices that perpetuated the problem.

GREAT EXPECTATIONS/
GREATER DISAPPOINTMENTS

"I think I'm about to be fired, and I'm so over my head in debt, I'm ashamed to tell anyone—even my family. I'm sure that I'm the only one who is having these problems."
—*thirty-eight-year-old car salesman*

One of the first things that most of us have to acknowledge is that few people have been lucky enough to come out of the last few years unscathed. Just about everyone is having problems. Understandably, someone who is feeling emotionally stressed out, financially "maxed out," and physically worn out often finds it difficult to relate to others' problems. It's easy to get so wrapped up in your own struggles that you fail to notice what the other guy is going through. So instead of sharing our experiences and learning from each other, we become convinced that our plight is unique and embarrassed and afraid of what others will think.

We become convinced that nobody else can identify with our own situation. Frequently, we may even find ourselves feeling envious of others who we believe are somehow more settled or more secure. This tendency to disconnect from others is self-defeating, because most of us are struggling. Our professional and/or personal paths are generating levels of disappointment that few of us could have anticipated.

Most of us are frustrated, most of us are confused, and most of us don't know what to do about it. Take this simple expectation/disappointment inventory. How many of these questions speak to your current dilemma?

1. Are you worried that success is eluding you and that the type of life you envisioned for yourself will always be beyond your grasp?
2. Do you feel that you have not been adequately rewarded financially for the amount of effort you have put into your work?
3. No matter how old you are, do you feel that other generations have had it "easier"?
4. No matter what your status, occupation, or earnings, are you unable to afford the kind of life (home, furnishings, clothing, entertainment) that you believe would reasonably reflect your level of professional accomplishments?
5. Are you chronically anxious about the future?
6. Do you feel that you were "sold a bill of goods" about what your life would be like if you paid your dues?
7. Have you created your own personal debt monster?
8. Is it impossible to imagine changing gears right now— i.e., cutting back on the amount you work—without jeopardizing everything you have struggled to accomplish?
9. Are you ashamed or embarrassed that you are not as successful as you anticipated?
10. Do the demands of your work make you physically or emotionally unavailable to those you love?
11. Is your body telling you via real symptoms (gastric disturbances, headaches, depression, panic attacks, etc.) that you can't keep living the way you're living?
12. Is your entire peace of mind riding on the belief that "tomorrow" your life will be very different?

ALL THE RIGHT MOVES?

"When I was going through the process I thought I didn't make a single wrong move. Now, sometimes I feel as though I didn't make a single right move."
—*Geoff, thirty-nine, computer franchise owner/manager*

From the first time we sat in a guidance counselor's office at the tender age of fifteen or so, we were told that we could shape our careers depending upon the choices we made. Certain words and phrases became a part of our working vocabulary. We were told about career "directions" and "paths." We were asked to make "choices" and plan "strategies." We were given techniques to help us judge whether or not we were "on target."

Many of us, right then and there, began to plan a course of action based upon those methods and attitudes that best reflected our abilities and our own personal style. All of this implied a structured methodical approach toward shaping one's life. And, if you are like most people, you liked the feeling this gave you; you liked having a sense of being able to map out your own future.

But if you have taken the time to make a careful plan and "done everything right," everything necessary to implement it, you expect to see results. You assume that with enough effort, your plan will move ahead, right on schedule. If that doesn't happen, it leaves you confused and uncertain about what to do next. When one has invested valuable time and energy into making something work, it is difficult to change direction. Giving up certainly doesn't seem like a viable option. Instead, you may blame yourself, assuming that you did something wrong or you didn't try hard enough. So you try harder . . . and harder . . . and harder.

That's when the "plan" takes over and develops a life of its own. Eventually you lose that sense of being able to shape your life, of being in charge of your own destiny. Instead, your day-to-day existence develops a pattern over which you seem to have little control. Ultimately it seems as though the only workable solution is to put your "real" life on hold.

2

Putting Your Life on Hold

◀

IF YOU ARE LIKE MOST PEOPLE, YOU CARRY WITH YOU, IN YOUR mind's eye, a clear picture of exactly what you need in order to be happy—how much money you need, what kind of job you need, and what kind of living conditions you need. Enough money, the right job, a satisfying personal life, emotional and physical well-being—our goals concern themselves with these issues.

Whether it's the first home, the first million, or the first real vacation, typically most of us see ourselves achieving our specific goals and finding the happiness connected with them at some magical "tomorrow point." In our imaginings, once we reach this golden place, everything will work perfectly—all the bills will be paid, we will finally live in the house we deserve; we will drive a car that accurately reflects our desired persona; and we will own clothing that makes the appropriate statement about who we are and what we have achieved.

As soon as we reach our goals we expect to be able to devote more energy to our personal relationships, improve our social lives, spend time with our children, deal with our bad habits, communicate with our loved ones, and generally improve the quality of our lives.

Consider the following goals told to us by several of the men and women we interviewed:

"As soon as I make partner, then I'll be able to set my own hours, become less stressed, take care of my health problems, spend more time with my family. . . ."

"I owe a ton of money, but I figure once I can get K Mart to place an order, my worries will be over. . . . K Mart can solve all my problems. You know how many K Marts there are?"

"Once the reorganization happens, and the business gets more stable, I'll be able to delegate more. That will give me more time to do what I want. I'd like to do some of my own writing, for example."

"As soon as trading picks up, I'll be able to take care of the credit cards and put some money aside."

"We have to sell the apartment, for a profit. That way we'll be able to buy a house and move. This is a necessity. If we don't get more space, this marriage is doomed."

"I want f _ _ k you money, plain and simple. That way I
can get out of here and forget that I ever had to do this for
a living."

These goals say as much about a present condition as they
do about hopes for the future. What all of these people are
revealing is that today, in the here and now, they are experiencing extreme dissatisfaction with their lives—they are feeling overworked, frustrated, angry, powerless, and insecure.
They are having problems with their relationships, with their
families, with their health, and with their finances. But instead
of dealing realistically with their dissatisfaction, they are pinning their hopes on goals that may or may not be achieved.

It seems almost subversive to question goal-oriented behavior since we've all been encouraged to devote time and energy
to formulating our goals, defining our goals, clarifying our
goals, and reevaluating our goals. But the people who have put
their lives on hold have typically carried this behavior pattern
too far. They have allowed their goals to become all consuming. Instead of being goal oriented, they have become goal
obsessed.

SACRIFICING FOR THE PROMISE

These people are living their lives based almost entirely on
expectations. Doing this means making lopsided trade-offs—a
life that is fulfilling on a day-by-day basis in exchange for an
illusory tomorrow. In short, when we put our lives on hold, we
forget about today. Today loses all meaning except insofar as

it affects tomorrow. We tell ourselves that it's okay to be miserable today, okay to be depressed today, okay to be overworked today, as long as our current condition is part of the sacrifice for an idyllic tomorrow—the perfect tomorrow.

End result: We are living on promises.

SACRIFICING YOUR PRESENT

Living on promises can't help but adversely affect the way you view the world and the way you interact with it. The first requirement for a balanced life is living in the here and now. By definition, putting your life on hold means that you have to give up a great many here-and-now satisfactions. You may find that your day-to-day existence is barely tolerable.

If you are pinning all your hopes on a brighter tomorrow, your life may be typified by the kinds of sacrifices you have made in the hopes of securing your goals. Unfortunately, the following scenarios may seem all too familiar.

Although you appear to be functioning well to the outside world, just below the surface you are in a constant state of anxiety; you have come to accept this as being part and parcel of your current condition.

"Remember the movie, *I Wake Up Screaming*? That could be the title of my biography. It used to just happen every couple of weeks, but now most mornings I wake up with an incredible anxiety attack. Sometimes it goes away by noon. But lots of times I'm uncomfortable for the entire day. The first couple of times I thought I was going to have a heart attack. I actually went to the emergency room. What causes it? The uncertainty—about the future, my bills, my choices. But I can't really spend too much time thinking about it. I'm just going to have to live with this.''

—Jeff, forty-one-year-old mortgage broker

Anxiety is the characteristic that most clearly defines the person who has put his or her life on hold. Rapid heartbeat, shortness of breath, a sense of dread, a knot in the stomach are symptoms of a level of anxiety for which nothing could have prepared us. It doesn't seem fair to you that someone could have worked as hard as you have and still be worried.

Probably the worst thing about worry and anxiety is the amount of psychic energy it takes to push these sensations away and continue functioning. It's exhausting and it takes a heavy toll, making you even more tired, which makes you even more anxious.

You are out of touch with what you are doing, feeling and being on a day-to-day basis.

By definition, someone who is living only to hear the good news—that the deal has come through, the money has come through, the promotion has come through, the sale has come through—is not able to relax enough to get any pleasure from the present.

You are not always in the world of the living. You are often so fatigued and drained that you are numb; you are usually so stressed that you cannot relate to your immediate environment in any meaningful way; you are sometimes so distracted that you cannot connect with your friends and family in a human fashion.

It's becoming increasingly difficult to maintain your facade of "everything's going great." Doing so is becoming more and more of a strain, and the sense of living a lie is beginning to catch up with you.

Although you realize that something is terribly wrong, you don't want to stop and acknowledge the depth of your disappointment or all of the ways in which your life is not satisfying. If you did, all of the bad feelings might rush in and engulf you. So you block out much of the reality you are experiencing. This is understandable. When the pain, emptiness, or conflict of the present is too great to be addressed, we stuff it down so deep and cover it up so well that we almost don't feel it at all. This is called denial.

To a certain extent, every single one of us is always in denial. Otherwise, addressing all of the harsh realities of day-to-day life would be overwhelming. We develop emotional survival techniques; we put up walls, thus shielding ourselves from the pain and anxiety. Denying pieces of the reality we experience is our way of defending ourselves so that we can function. Most of the time this is not a conscious choice. It is a process that occurs almost automatically to protect us from feelings that we do not have the skills to handle. In short, denial is often the way we handle traumas that are more than we can bear.

But when we are using denial as a means of blocking out so much of our reality that we cannot see what we are doing or how we are contributing to our own problems, denial becomes self-destructive. That's what too many of us are doing. We're hiding our own truth, and we're covering up how we feel. This means lying and rationalizing our positions, even to ourselves.

You only see success in the future tense. No matter how much you have accomplished, no matter how high a level you've reached, professionally or personally, success as you envision it for yourself is something that you have yet to attain.
Many of us can identify with the feelings of Delores, a thirty-eight-year-old businesswoman, who says she wakes up every morning worrying that she's a failure. For as long as she can remember, she has been struggling with the promise of a future success. When she was thirty, Delores, a single parent, said, "If I could only start my own business in my own home so I wouldn't have to worry about child care, I'd be satisfied." Without any financing, Delores, a talented artist, started a small graphics company. The business did well, but it was "too small" and it didn't give her any sense that she could sit back and rest on her laurels; it wasn't enough to make Delores feel successful. So she went after more business, added one employee, and then another.

At this point the business was growing well, but Delores's home was a wreck—filled with filing cabinets and office equipment. When she woke up in the morning, she wanted to feel like a success, but instead she felt like a person out of control. So she got a bigger place, which added to her overhead, and took away from her income so she had to do more business. That made her feel as though she was always struggling. Delores believes that when you are a success, you should not have to struggle.

Through it all, Delores has continued with her own art. She has illustrated a couple of children's books, which were well reviewed, and she was in one small show. Delores acknowledges that, though this is nice, it's not what she would call "really successful."

Marty, a forty-year-old doctor, also worries about being a failure. He says: "I know to the layman just being a doctor automatically confers a certain connotation of success, but it's different when you're on the inside. I understand the gradations of success. I know who went to medical school at Harvard and who went to Grenada. I know who had a residency in a large teaching hospital and who was a resident somewhere in the Poconos. And I know who is making really big bucks and who is forced to spend weekends covering for other doctors. I'm in research with a university—I'll never get rich unless I get famous.

"These things didn't use to bother me as much. But they bother me now. Not that I expect to win the Nobel or anything. But I know that I haven't achieved as much financially as lots of people I went to school with, and of course it bothers me. My cousin, for example. He's a real jerk, and he's a dermatologist. But he's socking it away. Sure, I get published and I get grants and all that, but I've never had a really big grant. I'm a small potato in the research field, and it bothers me. But I'm banking on getting a bigger grant: that's going to make the difference in my life."

Objectively, both Delores and Marty have so many reasons to feel successful. Delores built her business against tremendous odds; Marty graduated from one of the finest medical schools in the country and is involved in work that any outsider would consider important and prestigious. Yet neither of them is able to stop long enough to take justifiable pride in his or her accomplishments.

To appreciate Delores's and Marty's distress, one has to understand the high expectations they have placed upon themselves. Delores wants to be able to stay home with her children, run a small money-making business, and become a major artist. Marty wants to do his own research in an academic atmosphere far from the pressures of big business. And he wants to get rich. It's easy to see why they are not meeting their own expectations. It's harder to understand why they are feeling genuinely disturbed by it, and why they fail to understand that they are successful.

People who put their lives on hold typically have set high expectations of what they should achieve. Frequently, they have careers that they find fulfilling. If it were not for their high expectations, they would be feeling very content. ''The promise'' looms so large in their minds that it blocks them from appreciating what they are and what they have. Instead, they often feel an absolutely unwarranted sense of shame, based upon a distorted perception that tells them they don't have as much as some of their peers.

These people frequently examine what others have achieved compared to what they have achieved; they examine what others own compared to what they own. In fact, they compare everything—cars, homes, furniture, clothing, degrees—and they discover the distressing truth: Someone is always going to have more or better.

Anything that is not contributing to moving you closer to your goals is seen as an irritant. You have no emotional energy left for developing any outside interests.

Some examples: Your best friend from college is getting

married this weekend. Instead of being full of joy, you're annoyed. Not annoyed at him for getting married, but annoyed that he's getting married this weekend. Why this weekend? Why now? You have so much to do . . . catching up, cleaning up, getting ahead. If only he could wait six months. The wedding will shoot a whole day of work . . . and there's the party the night before—another half day lost. Don't they understand that you can't afford that kind of time? The commuting time, the time you'll lose if you get to sleep too late or if you have too much to drink and can't function effectively the next day. Who can afford this now?

Another family function? What a colossal waste of time, especially now when you're under so much pressure. Do you risk being the black sheep of the family by not going? You know how your family feels about "family." Family comes first, last, and in between. How incredibly provincial of them . . . how shortsighted. Don't they understand that the last thing you can afford to do right now is stop to take a day off for something like this?

Your focus is so strong that if you veer for a moment you get anxious and irritated. You're giving 1,000 percent to your goal and that leaves zero for anything that doesn't bring you any closer to that goal.

Whether it's a wedding, a family function, or a high school reunion, you go because for some set of twisted reasons you can't get out of going, but you're angry. Angry that it had to be now. Angry that they're not more sensitive to your needs and more understanding. Angry that they've actually pressured you into showing up by making sure you know exactly how hurt they would be if you didn't come. You are so angry that you can't imagine enjoying any of it.

The really strange thing is that once you get there, as the hours pass, you begin to loosen up and actually start to have a good time. You laugh, share a story or two, try eating something you've never had before, talk to someone you've never talked to before. By the end of the evening, you're really glad you went. In fact, you vow you're going to do things like this more often. The break is good for you; it gives you some perspective, some clarity. It will probably make you far more efficient on the days you are working.

You passively depend on someone or something to force you out of yourself. Within weeks, you've fallen back into the same pattern and the same kind of thinking. You are once again irritated at the thought of breaking your momentum.

You believe that if you make any attempt to cut back and give your goals less time, less energy, less devotion, it will bring the whole ''thing'' crashing to the ground.

You never stop working. If you are not actively engaged in working, you are thinking about working. When the typical workday is done, long after others have called it quits, you can still find people to call, leads to follow up, not to mention paperwork and other odds and ends that need your attention. If you go away for a day, you call your office repeatedly or you check in with your machine at ridiculously short intervals. Your attitude is closer to that of a knight with a quest than that of a person preoccupied with work. Each project becomes a personal crusade, each deadline a matter of life and death. You behave as if your psychic energy is the glue that is holding all this together. Your dedication borders on the spiritual.

There is an element of superstition here. You believe that if you stop concentrating, if you lose your focus for just a minute, the whole thing will disintegrate.

No matter how unhappy you are with your life, you truly believe that your priorities—work first—are appropriate and necessary for this stage of your life, but you have placed no realistic guidelines on how long this stage is to continue before you shift priorities.

"I really can't continue doing this much longer. It's wiping me out. . . . Next month, if everything goes well, I figure I'll take some time off, but that's what I said last month."

—Vince, forty-two, restaurant owner

Realistic is the key word here. We are unable to be realistic because there are so many conditions that we are taking into account: "if things go well," or "if the money comes in." So instead of saying, "Today I will realize that my health is my first priority, or my children need me more than my work," and behaving accordingly, we gaze into "tomorrow" land, the land of promise.

Vince's wife told us that at least once a week she tries to get her husband to make some kind of commitment that will limit the hours he works. She said:

"He complains constantly. Yet he does nothing about it. When I ask him how long he is going to continue working at this killer pace, he gets angry at me. He doesn't want to think about it, and he certainly doesn't want to talk about it."

Most of us started out working with the understanding that although it might be difficult, if we did everything right and worked as hard as we could, ultimately we would be successful. The struggle would be worth it. The investment of time and energy would pay off, and we could live happily ever after.

What we are discovering is that we may have understood incorrectly, and that a large part of the reason why we are unable to be realistic about our future is that our understanding is built upon a myth. This is something none of us wants to face. So we continue forward in the face of all logic, hoping against hope that a miracle will occur.

Let's face it: When we behave this way, we are a little like the card player who, despite his losses, continues to return to the casino night after night. He is certain that it is just a matter of time before his system pays off. Of course it can happen, but he is gambling with his life and the odds are terrible.

You recognize that there is no balance in your life, but you have lost the ability to pace yourself.

Balanced men and women lead balanced lives. That sounds so simplistic but it's true nonetheless. Someone who is living in the here and now would insist on a life in which there is a time for work and a time for play, a time for others and a time for oneself. Although in theory that's what you want for yourself, in practice that's not how you behave. While you are always interested in pushing forward toward your goals, you are rarely interested in anything else.

Even if you love your work, you know that you should start to be more measured about it all. You realize that you don't have a real life, a balanced life—the life you want. You say that's what you want for yourself, but when it comes to apportioning your time or your thoughts, you don't seem to be able to change your pattern.

**Your sense of what it means to be good to your-
self has become very distorted.**

One example: Tom, a thirty-one-year-old lawyer, assured
us that he never let his discomfort get so acute that he couldn't
handle it. He said:

"Sure I've spent nights napping on the office floor because
I have to get something done, but I don't let it go overboard.
When my body starts throbbing, I insist upon going home.
When I'm so tired that I can't move, I have this little therapy
that I do. I fill the tub with ice-cold water and ice cubes. I
make myself a protein drink and I get into the tub. Eventually
the pain goes away. Once I hit my bed, I'm asleep in seconds.
And the next morning, I'm as good as new."

Most of us are not as extreme in our remedies as Tom.
But many of us have lost all sight of what it means to be
good to ourselves. A number of people we spoke to cited
shopping binges as a way of being good to oneself; others
spent a fair amount of time talking about "large quantities of
chocolate."

It would appear that many of us are so tired and exhausted
that we have to do something, anything, to feel better. The
remedies range from the bizarre, as in Tom's case, to the
self-destructive, as in the case of those whose shopping sprees
have run up their credit cards, or whose food binges have run
up their weight.

**Even though you view yourself as someone who
wants to make a contribution to society, you see
your contributions as happening some time in the
future.**

A long time ago, probably when you were still in school,

you felt you could make a difference in the world. Even though you were only one voice, you wanted that voice to be heard. Making a difference in the world was a priority. Remember how important it once was to you to save the trees, promote cruelty-free products, or protest the inhumane treatment of political prisoners? Remember how you gave whatever time and money you had to the people and causes you believed in? Remember how you told yourself that when you got into the real world and started making real money, you would be able to make even more of a difference?

Then you failed to get involved with a political campaign for the first time, or you failed to keep your contributions up to date. Before you knew it, you were totally sidetracked by your own personal quest and you were losing sight of the bigger picture that was once so important to you. By now, you may not even be in the picture any more, but that doesn't mean you don't want to be. Who has the time? Or the money? With so many bills to pay, every dollar out seems like a small fortune.

Sometimes you try to make yourself feel better by telling yourself that the work you do is in itself a contribution to society, but that doesn't make you feel good for very long. When you see those guys from Greenpeace hanging off oil rigs, or the throngs at political rallies, you shrink back, feeling the emptiness of a life that has lost sight of the bigger issues. You vow you'll make up for this temporary period of self-focus. You vow that as soon as you have a few extra dollars, you'll send them where they can make a difference . . . or you'll do some volunteer work again . . . or write a letter to your local paper . . . but the clock keeps ticking and that day has yet to come.

SACRIFICING YOUR PERSONAL LIFE

Nothing is more indicative of a balanced life than satisfying and fulfilling personal relationships. In theory, just about all of us put a priority on intangibles such as love, friendship, and social interactions, but in practice you may have put your personal life on hold in one or all of the following ways:

You may feel forced to shortchange your loved ones, expecting them to understand that you plan to pay them all back at some future date.

When you think about your work schedule and what it is doing to those closest to you, you can't help being aware of the ways in which they are suffering. You rationalize by telling yourself that some day you will make it all up to them. In the meantime, you expect them to be supportive and understanding in the following ways:

• You expect your children to make few demands and to understand that your goals might ultimately bring more for them and financially enrich their lives, even though right now you are frequently unavailable, either emotionally or physically.

• You expect your partner to ask little, continue to be supportive, and not feel neglected or hurt even though you have little left to give to a relationship.

• You expect your partner to understand that you have little libido. Nights you're exhausted; mornings you barely have the strength to down a cup of coffee.

• You expect both your children and your partner to understand that you are unwilling to plan ahead; this affects all family leisure time including holidays, vacations, and weekends.

• You expect both your children and your partner to understand that you don't have the emotional energy to pay attention to details or to communicate with them about the details of living.

Your main source of recreation is crashing in front of the television.

"When I get home, I'm so tired I can barely stay awake through the news."

◄

"My girlfriend would like to go out more. I can't do it. Watching television is about all I'm good for."

◄

"I don't have the energy to go seek entertainment so the entertainment that comes to me is totally important. It's pathetic how much I look forward to my television set—a rerun or a preempt and I'm destroyed. On a day-to-day basis, I'm so depleted, television is all I have to look forward to."

Total exhaustion is the most common complaint of the person who is totally goal oriented. So what better way to tune out our anxieties and kill time than to crash in front of the TV while we're waiting for the day that we will have the strength to do something more productive in our spare time?

Whether it's Barbara Walters or Arsenio Hall, CNN or "Wheel of Fortune," television is different from other leisure activities. It's not like sports, gardening, reading, or chess— all of which require participation. Television allows the viewer to slump on the couch and space out. Although some may say that television gives little, it asks even less.

What happened to all the things you wanted to do, all the activities you were interested in pursuing further—music, tennis, golf, climbing, hiking, biking? What happened to spending time with friends, family, children? What happened to your zest for life, your desire to live life to the fullest, to do as much as possible, enjoy as much as possible?

Sex is no longer the priority it once was; either it takes too much time or it takes too much energy.

No matter what your marital status, you have less libido than you think is appropriate for your age and your stage of life. Who can think about sex at night when every muscle in your body is crying for sleep? And the mornings are out of the question. There are so many things on your mind, so many anxieties, and so many unresolved issues that desire is diminished rather than burning.

Typically most of your friends have problems that directly mirror your own and you have lost contact with those with whom you shared nonprofessional interests.

Remember when you had outside interests? And friends

who shared them? Remember when you chose your friends because they were supportive, understanding, and fun—not because they were good contacts, or had useful business information? Now when you see some of these old friends, you have nothing to talk about because they can't relate to your situation, and you have lost interest in everything else. You don't have the psychic energy to let anything else into your brain right now. It literally feels as though there is no room. It wasn't always like that. Remember when you prided yourself on your renaissance thinking? Then, you read every section of the newspaper, not just the sections that pertained to your immediate struggle.

Now you're so busy networking that you have no room in your life for friends who are not also business associates. And all you do together is talk about business. Sometimes this can make you nervous or reluctant to share too much. Even though you and these friends may gripe together about all the work-related problems you share, you still have to be careful about appearing too weak or wimpy. You still have to maintain a facade.

If you are single, you are so focused on work that you rarely have time either to date or to develop a new relationship. As a result, there is an accidental quality to the ways in which romantic partners enter your life—and often with disastrous results.

By now, if you are unattached, it's probably overwhelmingly apparent that your life-style is not conducive to finding or forming a solid relationship. Whether you're male or female, you are simply so involved in your work that you don't have the necessary time or energy for dating. Perhaps, if you're a man, you also feel that you're not earning enough to offer anything substantial to a mate; you may not even feel that you have enough money to date in a style that you find acceptable. If you're a woman, you may be concerned that you are so wrapped up in your professional image that you are frightening men away.

Yet you ache for a relationship. Someone to hold you at night and make you feel like a human being. Someone who will listen to everything you are going through and be supportive. Everyone wants someone like that.

Since you are so involved in work, your life is unbalanced. And you may also have lost your perspective and your own sense of self-worth. You feel a real need for a relationship, but you don't have the time or emotional strength to search for an appropriate partner. Frequently this means that you are wide open to all the inappropriate matches that come your way.

The person next to you on the plane, behind you on the movie line, on the nearest exercise bike at the gym, even the person in the office across the hall—these people fall into your life because of happenstance. Yet you are so needy that you assign a magical quality to these meetings and invest your energies into turning them into real relationships.

It was meant to be, you tell yourself, it was no accident that we were both stopped at the same traffic light. It was karma, pure and simple. So you are often twisting and turning trying to keep a relationship alive with someone who is somehow unavailable or with whom you have so little in common that it's almost frightening. But you go for it, telling yourself that it's divinely blessed . . . until the bottom falls out.

SACRIFICING YOUR HEALTH

Enough exercise, a healthy diet, adequate sleep, and emotional balance—all of these play a significant role in maintaining a way of life that helps protect one from illness. We all know this, and yet there is a tendency to put one's health on a back burner. If you are sacrificing your health. . .

Typically you have one or more of the following stress-related physical symptoms:

tension headaches
digestive disorders
insomnia
skin problems
stress backaches

Stress is frequently also a contributing factor in one of the following behavior problems:

excessive drinking
smoking
drug use
compulsive eating

Stress may also be causing you to experience emotional outbursts or mood swings such as:

depression
anxiety attacks

panic attacks
temper tantrums
crying jags

Instead of viewing these symptoms as your body's way of warning you that something is not right, you see them as being an accepted part of the process and see it all as something that will work itself out when your circumstances work themselves out.

As we interviewed people for this book, one of the things we found most amazing was the cavalier attitude with which they reported physical ailments and addictive behavior they felt were stress related. "It goes with the territory" was a phrase we heard time and time again as people described stomach ailments, drinking problems, and crippling migraines.

Among the younger people particularly, some of these severe complaints were viewed almost as a badge of courage. On some level, many indicated a belief that you weren't really a "player" unless you belonged to the fraternity of those in pain. So they clutch their bottles of Zantac and Maalox; they wave their prescriptions for Prozac and Valium; and they cope with their hangovers and their tremors. In short, the amount of emotional and physical punishment they were prepared to accept in the name of "working for the future" was mind boggling. Typically they were experiencing a fatigue that they describing as "numbing."

This inappropriate attitude toward one's emotional and physical health is an excellent example of the denial process. It indicates how one can detach from what is being experienced in the here and now and fail to acknowledge reality—even if that reality has clear-cut physical symptoms.

SACRIFICING YOUR FINANCIAL WELL-BEING

Having a balanced life means having a balanced checkbook and being in control of your money. When you are living on hopes for tomorrow's windfalls, it's all too easy to disregard today's limitations. For example:

You may have fallen into a pattern of spending that is determined by your emotional state and have spent money excessively as a means of rewarding yourself for the amount of effort you have put into trying to achieve your goals.

"I work so hard, I deserve it." Among those interviewed, this was a phrase repeated time and again as our interviewees described their spending habits. Most of them deprive themselves on so many other levels that it's easy to understand why they feel as though they deserve to buy themselves treats. The problem is that many of them can't afford it.

"I work too hard to deprive myself. When things get really awful, I close the door to my office and read catalogues. If I see something I like, I call the 800 number, order it, and charge it. I have it sent to the office. Then a week or so later, this package arrives. I've usually forgotten all about it. So it's like a surprise present. I give myself presents. It's my reward.''

—Maggie, a public relations specialist

"My last job, I worked so hard that I used to be numb by the time I got home. If I saw something I liked in a store window, I wouldn't think twice about running in and buying it on a whim. I had so little pleasure in my life that I figured I deserved it. During those years my primary recreation was shopping. Whenever I had a spare minute I would run into Saks. I ended up with one hundred fifty-two pairs of shoes and forty-eight pairs of boots. That's really crazy. I was a radical political organizer during the Vietnam War, and I ended up owning almost as many pairs of shoes as Imelda Marcos.''

—Diane, a lawyer

"My first mink . . . I walked into a store at lunch, saw a coat that looked appealing, said, 'Thank you very much. I'll wear it home.' I didn't even want to bother with the monogram: I needed it right then. Of course I couldn't afford it. I just figured I deserve it.''

—Joan, a designer

"I buy stereo equipment. . . and computer equipment. Do I need it? No. Do I want it? Damned straight. I figure it's the least I can do for myself. I deserve it—you know what I mean.''

—David, a doctor

"Restaurants are my downfall. After a killing day who wants to eat at home? I spend an amazing amount of money on food. I'm under such pressure that I figure I deserve to eat whatever I want, whenever I want.''

—*Alan, a financial analyst*

Working as hard as you do, you have little energy or time for economizing and spend an excessive amount of money on services.

When you leave for work by eight in the morning and you don't get home until eight at night, you frequently don't have enough energy to think about being economical and saving money. You certainly don't have time or strength to stop in the supermarket and get something to cook. So too frequently you indulge in salad bars and take-out Chinese food and restaurants. It doesn't seem that you're being extravagant until you add it up. Then you see what you spend. Lunches, for example. You can hardly start brown bagging it, but why should food cost so much?

And how about laundry and cleaning? Even if you wash your casual stuff—underwear and T-shirts—yourself, you still have to send out the good shirts and suits. Each shirt costs at least a couple of bucks, maybe more. After all, you're expected to look like a human being. When you feel like a human wreck, looking like a human being costs money. How can you stop long enough to get economical?

Believing that it was just a matter of time before you would be earning enough to pay back all of your creditors, you have gone heavily into debt. Your debts are now stressing you in one or more of the following ways:

• Your credit cards are charged to the limits and you are collapsing under the weight of the monthly payments.

• You moved into a house or apartment that is "probably too expensive" and you are bending yourself into a pretzel in order to pay your monthly mortgage or rent.

• You have borrowed excessively from parents, friends, institutions, and credit lines and are having difficulty making repayment.

• You are managing your credit cards and your mortgage, but you haven't paid all your taxes and you worry that it's just a matter of time before the IRS shows up at your door.

If you had savings, trust funds, or inherited money, you have dipped into it and perhaps gone through it. Now you feel ashamed and distressed for having done so.

It may not have been much money, but it represented security and some form of cushion. Perhaps you used it to start a business, or make a down payment on a mortgage. Perhaps you had to pay taxes, or just clear up bills. However you spent it, you told yourself that you would replace it as soon as possible. But you haven't been able to do so. Now you question your judgment. You had counted on that money to be there as your backup. But it's gone.

SACRIFICING YOUR FUTURE

There are so very many decisions one has to make all the time—where to move, when to move, what to save, how to spend, what to buy, what not to buy, what career move to make. What we decide about these issues and others will affect how we live tomorrow. On the most fundamental level, even a simple purchase such as any piece of furniture, from a bed to a rug, adds to our lives an object to which we will have to adjust. Larger considerations will have even more impact. In short, cause and effect works—what we do today makes a difference in how we will feel and live tomorrow. Here are some examples of ways in which you may be sacrificing your future:

Important decisions affecting what happens to you next week, next month, next year, and ten years down the line are made without sufficient consideration.

One might assume that someone whose thinking is tomorrow oriented might have a better chance at sound decision making, but this is not necessarily so. In fact, such a person is apt to make decisions that stem from two equally unreliable thought processes:

• Since "tomorrow" everything will be different, today's decisions aren't really important because they are only temporary. This kind of thinking, for example, can lead one into buying things that one intends to discard or moving into apartments that one plans to leave.

• One's current discomfort is so acute that he or she is looking for immediate relief and, in so doing, is failing to project all the necessary considerations and ramifications.

Because your goals leave no room either for others' reactions or for the twists and turns of the

universe, you are unprepared for a wide variety of unexpected events.

"I thought everything was going along, right on schedule, but my wife had a different idea. She said we had grown apart, and she left me for somebody who she said put a higher priority on a relationship. My world fell apart."

—Budd, forty-one, recently divorced

"I was doing great professionally, but the company was taken over. The new owners let me go with two weeks' severance. Now what?"

—a newly unemployed sales manager

When you formed your goals, you probably failed to take into account all the ways in which they could be thwarted, or all the ways in which others would affect you. Did you, for instance, take into account how the general economy would alter your plans? Did you fully recognize that your spouse or other loved ones could react emotionally and force you to alter your plans? Did you take into consideration the ups and downs of your particular industry?

When one is involved in one's own particular quest, it is all too easy to disregard what is happening in the rest of the world. This kind of thinking can prove to be calamitous.

SACRIFICING YOUR VALUES

So much has been written recently about putting more value and meaning in our lives. But most of us don't think of ourselves as shallow or superficial people. In fact, each of us probably has a decent grasp on what's really important, what really matters. We don't think of ourselves as being driven by blind ambition, and we wouldn't consider ourselves immoral or amoral in any way. Quite the opposite—we probably have a strong sense of values. However, if you have been giving everything you've got in an attempt to get ahead, chances are you have sacrificed some of your values in one of the following ways:

Your life doesn't reflect what you believe to be important.

On a day-to-day basis, your goals frequently eclipse your values. You don't spend as much time with the people who really matter to you as you do with those with whom you are networking for the sake of your career. More often than not, you devote more energy to issues that don't matter to you than to those that reflect your true values. Perhaps your need to succeed may even have forced you to do or say things that are totally opposed to what you believe in.

As far as money is concerned, you don't think of yourself as greedy; you don't really want that much for yourself. You know that when you get down to basics, who you are and how you think is far more important than how much you earn. Nonetheless, you have probably handled money in a way that doesn't mesh with the way you like to think of yourself. And, you can't help it—you think less of yourself for not earning more.

If you have children, you may not be setting the kind of example you want them to have. You may not have invested enough energy teaching them values that they will need to get through life. You have probably failed to give them a realistic attitude toward money and how to use it, and you know, in your heart of hearts, that one of these days you are going to have to do something to improve or change their attitude toward money and the objects money can buy.

How about your intellectual development and, even more important, your spiritual development? These are areas in your life that have probably been sacrificed for your goals.

Your identity and your sense of self are so totally wrapped up in your work that you have lost sight of who you are.

You have lost sight of who you are if:

• You feel most alive when you are involved with your work.

• Your sense of self-worth is overwhelmingly wrapped up in how well compensated you are for the work you perform.

• Your sense of belonging is totally tied up with the people you work with.

• You don't know what you would do if tomorrow you were forced to stop working or had to change careers.

• On holidays and weekends, you feel at loose ends, and you structure this time so that there will still be space for work-related activities.

ARE THESE SACRIFICES WORTH THE PRICE?

Sacrifices are made with the expectation that the payoff will be worth the price. But what about those situations in which the payoff is not worth the price? By definition, sacrifices that eat away at your existence are not good investments. A lesson we all need to learn: If you've been giving everything you've got and still not getting what you hoped for, it becomes increasingly evident that it's unrealistic to sacrifice your health, your family, your friends, and yourself for an illusory tomorrow.

3

Feeling Bad About the "Feel Good" Years: Myths That Failed Us

◥

"Of course I'm angry. I feel as if everybody lied to us. When I went to school, nobody ever told me there would be limitations."

—thirty-three-year-old programmer

"I think I can gauge how happy or unhappy most of my friends are by how much they believed *the big lie*."

—twenty-eight-year-old lawyer

"We were sold a bill of goods. And now we're suffering for it."

—thirty-two-year-old interior designer

How did it happen? Why did so many intelligent people develop expectations that would encourage them to put their

43

lives on hold? Why have so many of us been leading lives that are based on promises? Is it our own fault?

Those of us who now find ourselves frustrated and unhappy—were we just foolish, naive, gullible, maybe even stupid? How could so many people start out with such high expectations and end up with such major disappointments?

When we start thinking about these questions, we can't assume full responsibility; we need to take into account the larger picture. After all, we didn't form our expectations in a vacuum. What enabled us to create and maintain our own personal fiction was a constant sense of reassurance from the world around us that everything was going great economically. If everything was going great, and everyone was doing great, didn't it make sense that we should do great too?

The world was full of optimistic messages, and there was no reason not to believe them. Our dreams seemed logical, realistic, and attainable. All we had to do to reach our goals was follow certain hard-working routes, and the American dream would reward us. We heard these words everywhere—from our parents, from our teachers, from books, magazines, newspapers, television, even in campaign promises.

Unfortunately, we are now discovering, the hard way, that the majority of these messages were myths that have no real meaning for our lives. While it's foolish to beat up on ourselves for buying into a system that didn't deliver the goods, it's even more foolish to pretend that these myths, which were instrumental in the shaping of our world view, don't continue to hold power over us.

The myths and the messages contained within them are incredibly seductive. Throughout our lives they will have a tendency to resurface at regular intervals to tempt us with unrealistic promises. Unless we are going to spend our lives, Don Quixote fashion, tilting at windmills, we need to remember this: We must keep ourselves firmly rooted in reality and never forget all the ways in which we can be seduced by impossible dreams.

MYTH NUMBER 1:
THE ECONOMY WITH NO TOP END

For nearly three decades after World War II, the rise in American living standards was as reliable as a Maytag washer. . . . In the first decade following the war, young families moved into Levittown-style houses at the rate of 4,000 a day. In the next decade, auto production approached one million a month. And by 1975, Americans were buying enough wash-and-wear fabrics each year to cover the state of Rhode Island. The march of material prosperity created the easy assurance that each generation would live better than the last.

Today that has changed.

Wall Street Journal, May 1, 1989

Many of us formed our specific goals at a time when there seemed to be no limits to the growth of the American economy. The pie kept expanding, and as each generation reached adulthood, they claimed an even more valuable piece than the previous one—while preparing their children to do the same. It was un-American to assume that these expectations were unrealistic or unreasonable.

Then a funny thing happened on the way to the shopping

mall. Those of us who grew up believing "The sky's the limit" are now forced to deal with some unpleasant economic realities. In the words of Henny Penny, "The sky is falling." What this means is that, in all likelihood, the future growth of the American economy will be limited.

Here are some unpleasant facts that will markedly affect not only your economic well-being but that of your children:

• Downward mobility is not just a clever catchphrase. Unless something happens, it could turn into the dominant theme of the next twenty years. Researchers recently predicted that men who will be twenty-five to sixty-four years old in the year 2000 will have only a 34 percent chance of reaching a higher-ranking job than their fathers; 41.5 percent will meet, but not exceed, the level of their fathers' careers; and 24.6 percent will have lower-ranking jobs.

• Debt permeates the American economy. Let's face it, we all owe money. How much? Only you know how much debt you are carrying personally, but here are some numbers that could help you figure out what your neighbors owe. During the Reagan years, the national debt expanded to well over 3 trillion dollars. Business debt is another 3 trillion. And consumer debt (that's us) is about 2.8 trillion dollars.

• The rich have gotten richer, the poor have gotten poorer, and the middle class has gotten smaller and more financially frazzled. For example, in 1958, 58 percent of all American households could be described as middle class. In 1973, that number had decreased to 51 percent and by 1985, only 39.4 percent of all American households could be counted somewhere in the middle.

• Within the last ten years, income distribution has been

steadily shifting and now most of the money is in the hands of a very small wealthy minority—68 percent of the money is being controlled by 10 percent of the American households.

• During the eighties, while the typical millionaire was making out like a bandit, in real dollars the average family was losing ground. In fact, in 1987, the after-tax median family income was well below that of the late 1970s. For example, in terms of constant 1987 dollars, average yearly earnings rose from $17,062 in 1970 to a peak of $18,109 in 1972. By 1980, that number, adjusted for inflation, decreased to $16,699. And by 1989, it had further decreased to $15,968.

• For many young families, home ownership has changed from the American dream to the impossible dream—for those under fifty-five, the percentage of families owning homes has fallen. Since 1973, in the twenty-five to twenty-nine bracket, the percentage of young-family homeowners has slipped from 44 percent to 35 percent.

• Those people who own their own homes are facing a situation in which a scorchingly disproportionate amount of their earnings is being spent on monthly mortgage payments. According to *U.S. News and World Report*, a typical thirty-year-old male who bought a median-priced house in 1984 would have to devote 44 percent of his gross monthly income to carrying charges; in 1973, it was only 21 percent.

• For the growing number of property owners who are unable to find buyers for homes that have decreased in value, the dream of home ownership has changed into a nightmare that is effectively limiting their options and altering their futures.

• The only reason many average middle class families have been able to keep up with inflation is that so many extraordinary wives have entered the marketplace, thereby adding a second breadwinner; even with two incomes, many of these families are still not earning enough to meet their needs and are being forced to cope with the realities of inadequate child care, inadequate medical care, and inadequate leisure time.

All of this information points out that we might have to reckon with a changed world in which there is a limited amount to go around. Dealing with the prospect of limitations is never easy. No one wants to hear about it, and no one wants to believe it. It's human to want to maintain the expectation fashioned by yesterday's news—that if each of us works hard enough, pays his or her dues, and puts in enough time, eventually we will reach our goals. Unfortunately, clinging to that belief is setting us up for an untenable life.

MYTH NUMBER 2: HORATIO ALGER ALWAYS SUCCEEDS

Horatio Alger, the author of books such as *Fame & Fortune, From Farm Boy to Senator, Work and Win, Upward and Onward,* and *Rags to Riches,* is celebrated as offering a comforting thesis that virtue and industry are always rewarded. Many people say that this belief, which is deeply embedded in the American psyche, led them astray. Mark, a fifty-year-old art director is one such person:

> "I'm a product of the sixties; I'm very cause oriented. So when I started my business, I acted like it was a cause. I had

no financial smarts. I believed in the Horatio Alger concept—I thought hard work was the answer. If you work hard, surely goodness, mercy, and justice will prevail. If I did wonderful work, I assumed people would beat a path to my door. That's not life. That's fairy tales. I thought I would be rewarded for my work, people would pay me the fair price, and I would get ahead. It didn't work. I worked hard; I didn't work smart. That's a lesson I didn't learn until one day when I looked up and realized I didn't have a bank account. Nobody had rewarded me."

Mark is not alone in his attitudes. Horatio Alger is unarguably one of the most powerful images connected with the American dream. Books, television, magazines, and even presidents have invoked Horatio Alger as a symbol of all that one can achieve right here in America. Before discussing Horatio Alger, the larger-than-life myth, let's talk about Horatio Alger, the reality.

The real Horatio Alger was a Unitarian minister who was evicted from his New England parish because he was suspected of making overtures to young boys. He moved to New York where he quickly began to write his rags-to-riches tales. Most people living today have only heard about the Horatio Alger novels; few have actually read them. We assume the heroes to be hardworking young men who succeed as a result of their own labor. In fact, the typical Horatio Alger hero became successful not so much as a result of his own pluck and enterprise but from having the good fortune to meet a kindly older gentleman of extraordinary wealth. The older gentleman immediately takes a liking for the young man, rescues him from his uncertain fate, and bestows on him certain kindnesses that allow the young hero to succeed.

As for Horatio Alger himself—he was a struggling writer who went through a series of financial ups and downs—mostly downs. Unfortunately, he never saw the kind of financial success he wrote about.

Even more unfortunate is that so many people have modeled their entire life plan on the imagination of a man whose work reflected only fiction. For the most part, when we read novels we recognize the fictions for what they are. In the American consciousness, the fantasies of Horatio Alger have been been elevated to heroic proportion and imbued with a meaning and reality that they simply don't deserve.

Marcie, who was recently layed off from her job as associate producer of an educational television show, is a thirty-year-old woman who seemed to embody many of the qualities of the typical Horatio Alger myth.

At fourteen, Marcie ran away from a repressive home and struck out on her own. Living by her wits, she moved to another state where she managed to find a job, graduate from high school, and put herself through college with no family or outside financial help whatsoever. Right now, she says she is deeply distressed because she is unable to transform her life in the way she expected. Her most recent job, which ended because of cutbacks in the industry, was not particularly well paying, and she has no savings. She is currently working as a temporary word processor. She says:

"No matter what I do, I haven't been able to establish myself in the television industry. All the jobs I've had have been poorly paid. I live at a basic poverty level. I drive a car that's so old it's scary. I can afford few luxuries. I don't think

I'll ever be able to catch up to my peers. And I'm genuinely shocked that I haven't been able to succeed.

"I managed to get through my teens on my own, and go to college—I thought if I could do that, I could do anything. I was so sure of my life skills that I just assumed I would get ahead. I've done everything I know how, but it seems useless.

"Some of my friends tell me that I could be more successful if I only learned to play the game, but I've refused. I refused to cheat. I refused to use people. I thought the Protestant work ethic would just get me wherever I wanted to go: you know, work hard, pay your dues, but be relatively intelligent about it and you could do anything. Are you kidding? Who's going to hold you back? It's America, right? But it hasn't worked so far.

"I'm really stunned by my failure."

Realistically, at thirty Marcie is extraordinarily successful. She has managed to make huge inroads in a tremendously difficult and competitive industry. She has a large circle of supportive and loving friends. She has tremendous emotional resources and strengths. Yet, in her mind, she hasn't earned the money and reached the magical success she dreamed about. Sadly, her inability to meet her own expectations is affecting her self-esteem and her spirit.

MYTH NUMBER 3:
THINK AND GROW RICH
AND OTHER SELF-HELP CLICHÉS

"My parents were very influenced by EST and other positive-thinking types of philosophies. They really laid it on—all this stuff about attitude being everything. They didn't quite have me visualizing for success, but they sure told me that if I wanted something badly enough, nothing could stop me from getting it. All that stuff was a major lie that was fed to me, and a lot of my friends.''

—twenty-seven-year-old carpenter

''I grew up with the idea that if I wanted something badly enough I would be able to get it—almost as if the idea of wanting something was enough to make it happen. It sure hasn't turned out that way, but a part of me honestly believes that it's because I wasn't clear enough about what I wanted.''

—forty-two-year-old writer

''I'm part of the generation that was told we could 'write our own life scripts.' I'm doing okay, but I certainly don't have it all. My business has problems; I don't have a perfect social life. To the outside world, I look successful. But not only do I feel like a failure. I feel guilty because I blame myself.''

—forty-six-year-old architect

Although it is difficult to believe that books or seminars can have so much influence over someone's life, if you go anywhere in America and take a poll, you would be amazed at how many of us have had our thinking and consequently our lives shaped by some sort of self-help, you-can-conquer-the-world philosophy. At their best, these philosophies are very useful at helping us develop and maintain a positive attitude. At their worst, they play into our most unrealistic fantasies, encouraging a kind of childlike sense of omnipotence, allowing us to delude ourselves into thinking that we can do anything, simply because we want to. David is an excellent example of someone who built his life plan around the messages he received from reading the long-term best seller, *Think and Grow Rich*. He says:

"I'll never forget how it happened. I was twenty-two years old. I was bright, but I was also very confused and very impressionable. And that made me vulnerable. At the time, I was feeling a great deal of pressure from my parents and my peers to get on a clear success track—like medicine. I was about ninety percent decided to start medical school in the fall, but I was worried—all those years of school still ahead of me. One night I was having dinner with a former professor and his wife, and they were listening to me go on and on about my confusion over career paths. I was certainly interested in medicine, and I was really interested in having a secure profession with a secure income. But a large part of me wanted to become a writer. My primary concern was that being a writer would not necessarily produce a secure income.

" 'You must read *Think and Grow Rich* by Napoleon Hill,' my professor insisted. 'It's exactly what you need right now to sort things out.'

"Now, I had never read a self-help book before. In fact, I was virtually ignorant of the self-help phenomenon. I thought people who read these things weren't like me. I was a straight-A student. I hadn't dropped out and gone to California to find myself—or gotten into drugs to lose myself. I just couldn't get one hundred percent behind medicine as a career decision. The fact that a professor suggested the book made me more amenable to taking a self-help book seriously. I took it so seriously that all my decisions would change after reading *Think and Grow Rich*.

"I remember reading it for the first time on a flight from Miami to New York. I was so overwhelmed by the message of the book that I had tears in my eyes. It was on that plane flight that my thinking crystallized. I could be a success my way. I could have my cake and eat it too. I wouldn't have to worry about just having a secure income. I could be a writer and I could be rich—if I believed the message of the book. And I believed.

"I followed all the instructions. I made two sets of lists comparing the pluses and minuses of each path. Then I looked at the two lists—medicine versus writing. Medicine with all the minuses of long-term schooling versus writing with so many pluses and just a handful of minuses. The decision was no longer difficult for me. I would write, and one day I would be rich. No cadavers for me, no grueling internship and residency. I was headed for the top—my way.

"Possibly either choice would have led me to the same spot I'm in. But I certainly didn't get rich. I didn't even get solvent. At first I blamed myself. I thought I had done something wrong—wasn't enough of a believer. Although I hate to admit it, to this day part of me still wants to believe the message of *Think and Grow Rich*. It's hard to accept a world with real limits. I hate it. The thought of never being rich kills me; giving up that dream is just too hard. But the fact is that maybe twenty years ago you could think and grow rich. But right now all I can do is think and grow debt—twenty thousand dollars and still counting."

David is not the only person to be motivated by self-help

philosophies. There are many variations on similar themes, inspiring generation after generation of wide-eyed hopefuls who wanted to believe that there were simple formulas for success. Whether we're employing "persistence," "determination," or "visualization," it's comforting to believe that strength of will is the magic ingredient that will allow each of us to cross the barrier to greatness.

There is something terribly insidious in many of these books or seminars on life. The underlying message seems to tell us that once we have read the book, taken the seminar, or undergone the training, if we don't succeed, *we* haven't done enough. The burden of performance is always on the reader or the participant—never on the creators of the message. They are clever enough to shed themselves of all responsibility for our failures. No, if we don't succeed, it is because we did not "desire" enough, we did not exhibit enough "faith," we did not "visualize" correctly; we were lacking "imagination," "persistence," or "planning."

Obviously, this is blatantly untrue. While we all want to believe in miracles and wishful thinking, the unfortunate fact remains that we can't achieve success simply by applying the principles found in these oversimplified formulas.

MYTH NUMBER 4: REAL PLAYERS AND REAL WINNERS "GO FOR IT!"

"Go for it!" says your closest and most supportive friend, echoing one of the most successful advertising slogans of the eighties decade. "Here's to the winner!" goes the old bar cheer. "The world is divided into players and nonplayers," says the cynical salesman, adding, "and the players have all the fun." The swashbuckling personality who takes risks, the "player" who "goes for it" is an intrinsic part of the American dream. Let's not forget that before Ivan Boesky was an ex-con, he was an icon. He wrote books and delivered speeches such as his oft-quoted, "You can be greedy and still feel good about yourself" speech to the UC Berkeley School of Business. He appeared on major talk shows and was written about, frequently admiringly, in major magazines and newspapers. And people seem openly impressed with his capacity to "wheel and deal."

Even after Ivan Boesky ceased to be a "player," we watched the stock market soaring, and far too many of us saw all these guys with the many trappings of success and wanted to think of ourselves as players too. We read about the MBAs pulling down the six-figure incomes, and we watched the stock market soaring, and we wondered why we couldn't get a piece of it. Yes, let's admit it, we want to be "winners." It's human to want to be able to go for it and get it. And during the last decade, the world encouraged us to behave accordingly. It was more than just wanting to get rich quick. There was a straight-out appeal to the ego. Getting in the game gave us a sense of power, and it made us feel young and buoyant. Not having the resources to get in the game made us feel as though we were less worthy.

Margo, who owns a small clothing company, remembers:

"I would get these unsolicited calls and letters from people in investment companies trying to sell me on investing money. When they would call, it was embarrassing because I didn't have any money. I didn't know what to say. So I would lie and tell them I already had a broker. It made me feel that I wasn't worthwhile. Everyone seemed to be investing. When people talked about their investments, they sounded so proud, even when they talked about losing money—sort of like the act of putting money in proved something. It made them part of a special clique. Anyway, I didn't have enough money to join.

"Not being able to invest made me feel old. It was as if the world was filled with these young people who had money. I felt as if the world was passing me by. I felt as though because these people could afford to lose money, they could win. I couldn't even get in the game. It was a gamble, but you have to play to win. I couldn't play."

The world encouraged us to have more respect for players. In many instances, this need to get in the game has left scores of Americans clutching at their wallets and wondering how they could have been so gullible.

Walter, a New York doctor, says:

"I lost my son's college tuition. Stupidly. It was when everyone was making money on Wall Street. One of my patients, a guy who had really done well—a big spender, a big liver—kept talking about all the money he was pulling in. Anyway, he put me in touch with his broker. I figured he was a hotshot, and would give me good advice. My wife and I went to see him. We listened, and we decided to go for it. He put us into this limited partnership, but he didn't explain what that meant. He was with a big firm, the partnership was with a well-known company. It seemed safe. When the market went down in '87, I told him to get me out, to sell. Nobody told me that it would be hard to find a buyer. It's three years, and I still have this thing that I can't get any money out of. I don't know why I did it. Everybody was making money; I thought I could make money too.''

Ben, a thirty-six-year-old photographer, says what he remembers most about his loss was the Merrill Lynch commercial ''To know no boundaries.''

''I used to call my broker every other day and sing the song to him—as a joke—because he was burying me. It was a small amount, but it was all I had. I know why I did it. Having a broker, and investing money—it gave me a tremendous sense of freedom; it was like the commercial. I had a sense of no boundaries, and I felt like a real adult. Of course, I lost more than half of the money I put up. And start-up fees, brokerage fees, closing costs—all that took even more money. It was a foolish financial nightmare. I just thank God it wasn't more.''

MYTH NUMBER 5:
REAL ESTATE IS THE
ONE ''SAFE'' INVESTMENT

''You gotta buy land.''

Now that's a message we all heard. We heard it from our Uncle Harry and from our cousin Mo. We heard it from our parents and our children. We heard it from newspapers, magazines, television, and books, where we heard that we could buy it with ''no money down.''

We were told, loud and clear, that real estate was the only sure thing. During the eighties in many places, values were escalating so rapidly that we worried that if we didn't climb aboard the real estate merry-go-round, we would never, ever, have a place to call our own. And many of us behaved accordingly. Sophie, a New York graphic artist, says she remembers the frenzy when her apartment building went co-op.

"I was living in a two-bedroom rent-controlled apartment—my rent was six hundred eighty-five dollars a month. When we got the 'red herring' I had no intention of buying. Even if I wanted to, I didn't think I could afford it so I didn't even go to the first few meetings. But I would hear people talking in the elevator about how they were going to 'flip' their apartments. This was about 1984, and suddenly, overnight, everyone was talking about nothing but real estate.

"So I went to a meeting. There were all these lawyers and MBA types running around screaming at each other. Everyone talked about how much money they were going to make on their apartment. And it certainly sounded appealing. The insider's price on my apartment was sixty thousand dollars. The maintenance would be about six hundred fifty. You needed twenty percent down. Most people wanted to buy. And some people planned to sell immediately and reap a huge profit. If you couldn't come up with the twenty percent, there were people standing in line for the opportunity of buying your insider 'rights.' I was offered twenty-five thousand dollars for my rights. And if I wanted to buy the apartment and then resell it, I was told I would have no difficulty getting one hundred twenty-five thousand—which would mean a quick profit of sixty thousand. The notion of owning an apartment that was worth that kind of money was very heady. I remember one woman saying, 'My God, this is like winning the lottery.'

"Everyone I knew was telling me that I was stupid not to buy. There was this fear that everything was escalating so rapidly that if you didn't get in at that moment, you would forever be a renter. Only a short time before, it was okay to be a renter, but then suddenly it wasn't. Renters were subcitizens. They were left out of real estate conversations. Everyone knew that if you weren't buying, it was because you couldn't afford to, and it suddenly seemed humiliating.

"So I behaved like a 'big shot,' with a little help from my friends who loaned me most of the money for the down payment. The only problem was that with the cost of the rent and the cost of the mortgage, I couldn't afford the apartment. And I had to pay back my friends. So I quickly found a buyer. I actually sold the apartment for one hundred forty-five thousand, making an eighty-thousand-dollar profit. Sounds good. Right? Wrong.

"First of all, I had to pay taxes, which took a lot of the money. Then I forgot about finding another place to live that I could afford. I still couldn't afford to buy a place because the monthly mortgage and maintenance was too high. I couldn't afford to rent anything as nice as the apartment I left. In fact, I ended up renting a one bedroom, not as big, not as nice, for twelve hundred dollars a month. I work at home, and it wasn't big enough. So I had to go out and get a share in an office—another four hundred a month.

"Eventually I had to leave Manhattan. I now live in Queens. I spent so much money moving and I lost so much work time, that there is nothing left of the money I made. For me, the real estate boom is just a painful memory from which I have never recovered.''

Sophie was part of an unusual phenomenon that saw people, for perhaps the first time, speculating on their own housing. And because it was real estate, which had always been regarded as a sure thing, few people fully acknowledged the speculative nature of what they were doing. Consequently, a great many Americans now have painful memories. They wonder how they got in so deeply, and why nobody warned them about the consequences of overbuilding and no new baby boomers. In retrospect, it seems astonishing that the business and real estate pages, who were regaling us with prices that were going up, up, up, paid little or no attention to the shifting demographics. Most of us didn't realize that there were going to be fewer people to buy all our real estate.

There are dozens of variations on the real estate crisis. Here are just a few of them.

When the real estate boom hit, Greg, a Boston salesman, lived in a terrific rental apartment in a great neighborhood. His rent was so reasonable that it seemed foolish to try to buy a permanent residence; besides he couldn't really afford anything in the city.

''So I decided to get a condo at the shore. I figured it would serve two purposes—I would start building equity, and I could use it weekends and during the summer. It was beautiful, and I loved going there.

''But last year, business started falling off drastically. And I couldn't afford to pay my rent and my mortgage. So I got a tenant in the condo. The tenant's rent didn't cover my mortgage and maintenance—I lost about two hundred dollars a month. Then three months ago, the tenant moved. In the meantime, my business hasn't improved, and real estate has crashed. Every other house or apartment is for sale or for rent. No matter what I do, I can't find either a buyer or a renter. I have a seventy-five-thousand-dollar mortgage on the place. People tell me that if I reduced my selling price to forty-five or fifty thousand I might find a buyer. But I would have to cough up the difference to close off the mortgage. I don't have that kind of money. The worst part is that my parents cosigned on the mortgage, and I'm worried that the bank will foreclose and go after them. It's a nightmare.''

Marge and Dan bought the house of their dreams outside Los Angeles when the prices were at their peak. Within two years, Dan's job disappeared, and the only offer he can find is from a firm in Ohio. Dan says:

"We made an eighty-thousand-dollar cash down payment on that house. I'd be happy living there forever, but we have to move. The problem is the same one everyone is having. We can't find a buyer without reducing our price below what we paid and taking a big loss. This is a painful position, believe me.''

Dan is wrong about one thing. Everyone is not having the same problem. There are many men and women who feel that they will never have the problem of trying to sell a house— because they believe they will never, ever have the money to *buy* a house.

When Nancy and Jim first got married, they lived in an apartment in Marina del Rey; it was "perfect" for young marrieds who appreciated the fun of working in Los Angeles and living near the beach. Now they have two small children, and they are still living in an apartment. Although prices are a little lower than they were a few years back, they are still not low enough for them to afford to buy even a starter home. And they doubt if they will ever be able to. Jim says:

"Unless there is a miracle, there is no way Nancy and I will be able to buy a house. I guess maybe if we both find jobs in Kansas, maybe then . . . But right now, living here in California—which is where we have family—no way!''

MYTH NUMBER 6: THE LIMITLESS CREDIT CARD

Equipment, clothes, restaurants, gifts—it probably all seemed so innocuous at first. You were short of money, but you truly "needed" to go out to eat. So you used the first of many cards. And you liked the sense it gave you of being a person with resources, a person in control. So you used it whenever you needed something. And you began to need more things.

Then you discovered something incredible! The more you used your card, the more credit you received. Other people sent you cards—cards to use in department stores, cards to use at banks, cards that would be accepted everywhere—until finally you needed a new credit card holder for all of it.

At first it all seemed very easy. All you had to do was pay back a small amount every month. At first it seemed as though you had more credit than you would ever need. And besides, the more you used, the more your credit line in-

creased. But then you used more, and more, and more. The
payments got larger. They got harder to pay. Maybe you
even had to use your credit line to make the monthly payments. And then you ran out of credit. Now what do you
do? That is a very real and frightening thought that too many
of us are facing right now.

MYTH NUMBER 7: THE YUPPIE

Unfortunately, the glamour of this group obscures a more significant trend toward *downward* mobility among their peers. . . .
The median income for families in the 25–34 age bracket fell 14
percent (in constant dollars) from 1979 to 1983.
    —"The Year of the Yuppie," *Newsweek* Special Report,
December 31, 1984.

Remember when the yuppies took over all the restaurants?
It felt like it happened almost overnight. One night, there we
were in our favorite place, often at our favorite table, dining at
our leisure. The next night, there was a line of guys in suits
and women in suits and sneakers. It was as if someone had put
one of these couples in a Xerox machine and then run off
thousands of them, and they all had "discovered" *our* restaurant. There were so many of them, it was frightening. The
thought of waiting for an hour with these people was unac-
ceptable. No restaurant was worth that much wasted time.
    Why didn't the yuppies feel that way? They were like herd
animals—with their Akitas and their cordless phones; their

cappuccino machines and their take-out food; their health clubs and their running shoes; their expensive vinegars and designer barbecue sauces. Who were they anyway? Few people admitted to being one; most preferred putting down the "yuppiness" of the other guy. Some, like Sharon, a Miami-based photographer, took another tack in openly envying the so-called yuppies by saying, "I *wish* I could be a yuppie. Hey, give me some of what they've got."

Sharon was on to something, because one of reasons so few of us acknowledged our yuppiness is that few of us actually qualified as yuppies. According to the Newsweek article, while there were 60 million baby boomers, aged twenty-five to thirty-nine, in 1984 only 4 million of them were making the $40,000 or more necessary to qualify economically, and of that number only 1.2 million lived in cities.

We think that what most of us saw on the streets and in those restaurants were the men and women in their twenties who had their first hot job; they were a long way from having a comfortable life.

From our vantage point, instead of yuppie lives, most people in the eighties had "yuppie moments." We were yuppie hopefuls, yuppie impersonators. We were yuppies for a day or yuppies for a purchase, but not yuppies for very long.

One admittedly bitter thirty-four-year-old salesman summarized the period by saying:

"I have this friend, Eddie, who made a lot of money selling cars one year—1986. It was his year, and he bought everything. A BMW, a condo. Of course 1987 was a bad year, and he lost everything. Now he's driving a five-year-old Ford. The only thing he has left from it all are some designer coffees that he keeps on a shelf in his refrigerator. He never uses them because he says they are a reminder of his good year.''

MYTH NUMBER 8: FOR WOMEN ONLY—THE CAREER CRAZE, YOU CAN HAVE IT ALL, YOU CAN DO IT ALL, AND YOU CAN CHOOSE

By now, few women truly believe the myth of ''having it all.'' If you personally haven't experienced the sheer hell of trying to balance home, children, and job, you have surely watched a friend or two grapple with this impossible dream. You know that unless a woman has a massive and expensive support network, she is going to feel as though she is crumbling under the emotional and physical burdens of trying to work and raise a family. Yet, for a relatively long period of time, we were besieged with newspaper and magazine articles of ''women who have it all.''

Now we are inundated with articles telling us that more and more women are ''choosing'' to stay home with young children, thereby implying that the average woman has a choice of whether or not to go to work. The reality is that in today's economy, it's become almost impossible for a family to live with any level of comfort on one income, and women who have decided to stay home are learning that there is another price to pay. Kathryn, who had been employed as an advertising art director, says that not working has taken a toll on the relationship that existed between her and her husband:

''I was thirty-five when I became pregnant. My whole life

I looked forward to being a mommy and having a family. My husband was a little less sanguine, but he was prepared to support me emotionally and financially if that's what I wanted. So I left my job in my eighth month.

"David earned, and still earns, well over one hundred thousand dollars a year so I didn't think it was going to be such a problem. Well, the first difficulty was that the apartment we were living in was too small. So we moved to a house in the suburbs, which David loves. But then we needed a car. And then we needed more furniture. And then we had a great many medical expenses. And then I got pregnant again, unexpectedly.

"The kids are now two and four, and David is resentful, no question about it. Last year, he lost his job. Although he was only out of work for a couple of months, it scared him, and it scared me. We have no savings. The kids are in preschool programs which cost a good deal of money. There is no money left, and I can see David thinking: Why am I killing myself? Why doesn't she get off her butt and go back to work?

"I think that for me to get a job which would make it economically feasible to pay for help and the support system we'd need, I'd have to go back into the city. And I can't bear the idea of leaving the children for that long. It just kills me. But David says that right now, my attitude is killing him. He doesn't love his work. And he feels the pressure of supporting all of us has gotten to be more than he can bear. Our relationship is really suffering from this, and even my family has started in, telling me to go back to work. But I resent it. I want to stay home with my kids. I thought that's what it meant to be a good mother, and I don't see why I have to work."

Kathryn's story reflects but one of many ways in which

women have been confused by the messages they've received. She honestly believed that working or not working was an emotional choice, not an economic one. She, like many other middle class women, believed that she had the right to choose. She had the right to work, but she also had the freedom not to work. Now she realizes that the notion of choices may have just been an illusion.

MYTH NUMBER 9: THE NO-FAIL PROFESSIONAL PATH

"Don't believe all you read about MBAs making all that money. Sure, my boss makes a couple hundred grand a year, but the rest of us are pulling in sixty-thousand—and more than a few in my place are Harvard MBAs. And you have to work for that sixty-thousand. I try to be more balanced about it all, but it was recently pointed out to me that my position wasn't going to last unless I started burning the midnight oil. I do mean pointed out, not intimated. I was told flat out: stay late or pack up."

—thirty-two-year-old MBA

Doctors, dentists, lawyers, MBAs—those were supposed to be the golden professions. Scores of people grew up believing that if you were smart enough to get the degree, you would be immediately assured of earning an excellent living and being able to enjoy a comfortable life-style.

But listen to some people employed in these golden professions:

"My in-laws bought the house, my parents pay for the kids' schools, my wife works, and we still have to economize. Fortunately, my wife and I are both only children and our parents are able to help us."

—thirty-nine-year-old doctor

"The cost of setting up a dental office is prohibitive. I'll probably never have my own practice. Right now, I'm working in somebody else's dental office. Even so, it's tough getting patients."

—thirty-four-year-old dentist

Can this be true? Is it the professions, or is there something wrong with these specific people that makes them unable to automatically earn a good living?

It would appear that someplace in the last ten or fifteen years a tremendous shift has taken place in terms of what people are paid. The end result is a discrepancy in pay—not just between lawyers and gas station attendants, but between comparable occupations. In fact, according to recent studies culled from Labor Department data, as reported in *The New York Times*, "People who work in the same field and are of similar age and education are finding that their wages, once very close, now extend across a much wider range."

This implies that two people of the same sex, working in the same field, with similar education and background, can find themselves in completely different economic brackets. The *Times* cites electrical engineers in their early thirties, employed in Silicon Valley in California. In 1980, they would tend to earn within $12,000 of each other. By 1990, the spread had grown to $25,000 and sometimes more.

Among doctors, everyone was always aware that some specialties earned more than others, but now that spread can easily be $100,000 a year or more.

What this means is that some workers, seeing themselves being quickly outstripped by their peers, but unable for a variety of reason to earn more money, are becoming discouraged and depressed by what they may perceive as their own personal failure, rather than an unfortunate and unanticipated outcome of the economic policies of the 1980s. Others, trying to keep up, just work harder, hoping against hope that something will happen that will allow them to climb up the financial ladder. Edward, a thirty-seven-year-old doctor practicing in Boston, says:

"It depends on your specialty, and what state you're in. Some guys are making a lot of money—anesthesiologists, for example. But a lot of us are having a tough time. Many of my peers are like me—still paying off student loans. I still go on call for other doctors, for example. I've been practicing for ten years, and I still go on call for other doctors two weekends a month, just for the money. It's a killer for family life, but I have no choice."

Many professionals today are disappointed and not only with their earning capacity; they are also overwhelmed by the life-style burdens of their chosen professions. They are saying that they are working longer hours and are getting less and less in the way of personal satisfaction from their work.

Perhaps it is lawyers more than any other professional group who complain most bitterly about the expectations and the reality of their profession. Carl, a forty-year-old lawyer said:

"When I was growing up, two things influenced my ulti-mate career path. The most obvious, of course, was the Perry Mason myth. You know, the good-guy lawyer who brings justice. The second was not as altruistic. The richest guy on the block where I lived was a lawyer. I would watch him drive down the street in his big cars, new Cadillacs that he traded in every year, and I would see the kind of respect he got, and the kinds of benefits his kids got. And I decided then and there that I would be a lawyer. The fact is, often I hate what I do. I frequently find myself representing interests to which I'm far from sympathetic. And for me, the money is not what it was cracked up to be."

A recent survey by the American Bar Association tells us that dissatisfaction among lawyers is deeply rooted and widespread. Only slightly more than three in ten lawyers describe them-selves as being "very satisfied" with their work. According to *The New York Times,* the rest, "from all levels of seniority and kinds of practice, report that they are less fulfilled, more fa-tigued, more stressed, more likely to be in unhappy marriages and more likely to drink excessively than they once did."

In fact, a similar survey was conducted in 1984 when less than half of one percent reported consuming six or more al-coholic beverages a day. Among those responding to the cur-rent survey, the number having six or more drinks a day has now risen to 13 percent. This is doubly remarkable because alcohol consumption among the general population has been on a downswing.

Although money is always an issue, lawyers seem to be particularly distressed over the number of hours they have to put in. According to the ABA survey, in 1984 only 4 percent worked 240 hours or more a month. In 1990 that figure more than tripled to 13 percent.

MYTH NUMBER 10: YOU ARE THE MASTER OF YOUR FATE

"Sure I'm the master of my own fate, just so long as a larger fate doesn't get in my way."
—*Jack, thirty-four, computer specialist called into active service in the Gulf War*

We all want to cling to the belief that we have ultimate control over our lives, and to a significant degree we do. We have control over our friends, our love relationships, our sexual choices. We decide for ourselves what's right and what's wrong, whether we should vote Democratic or Republican, and who to invite over for the weekend. We are in control of what to say, what to wear, and what to eat.

However, we have very little control over government economic policies, the rise and fall of the stock market, Mother Nature, or international events—to name just a few. Large-scale occurrences can, and will, affect and sometimes force us to alter our plans, disrupt our lives, and undergo major financial upheavals.

Events such as the Gulf War or the recession, for example, left numerous Americans vastly unprepared for the emotional, physical, and financial consequences. Often there is little we can do and yet we are overwhelmingly affected.

When the stock market crashed, to cite another example, it left thousands without jobs. This dashed expectations and, in turn, contributed to a real estate downturn that diminished assets.

When you grow up in a climate of economic stability and relative peace, sharp changes in the economy or totally disruptive international events do not factor into your thinking. Nobody warns you; nobody prepares you. Everyone tells you to ''reach for the stars—you can achieve whatever you want.'' When people tell you to reach for the stars, they don't mention that you might get hit by a meteor. Few talk about the possibility of outside circumstances adversely affecting ambition. In fact, those people who worry about large-scale upheaval are usually ridiculed as being too negative or having doomsday personalities. And yet, how many of us can say that our ambitions and dreams have been left intact by the events of the last few years?

4

Who Are You and What's Really Important to You?

◢

SUCCESS BEGINS WITH A SENSE OF SELF

We all know what self-esteem is. We understand that self-esteem has to do with our sense of worth, our sense of identity, and our sense of personal competence. We recognize that self-esteem should come from within—a fundamental positive feeling at our core that says we're okay, that we have value as human beings—regardless of what we do or don't do for a living, how much money we make or don't make, how many possessions we own or don't own.

If you took any courses in basic psychology, you may remember that, for each of us, in the process of childhood development, self-esteem comes about as we internalize the many messages we receive about ourselves from the outside world. Ideally we receive positive messages and these contribute to giving us a strong inner sense of self, one that can withstand the normal trials and tribulations of everyday life. Self-confidence, self-reliance, self-acceptance, and self-worth—these are the components of a positive self-image. If someone has these kinds of positive feelings, he or she should be able to approach the world with a sense of surety.

Some time in the last few decades a profound disturbance seems to have taken place in the American psyche. All too often that core sense of self has been misplaced. Somewhere between Sunday school and our first jobs, many of us allowed our self-esteem and our self-image to become intertwined with our quest for success. Rather than recognizing the problem and working on our inner well-being, we have tended to turn outward and externalize our search for self. We forgot about self-esteem, self-confidence, and self-reliance and instead focused on image.

Certainly image is a fundamental part of our sense of self, but when our understanding of it is twisted around, we begin to believe that what we project to others will ultimately make us feel good about ourselves as well. When you feel good about yourself, you project that to your external environment. But can the opposite also be true?

Most of us remember when Billy Crystal appeared on "Saturday Night Live" in the character of Fernando and jested how he'd rather "look good than feel good." We laughed because of the comic superficiality of the character. But when you stop and think about it, is our view of the self terribly different? Isn't that how most of us feel right now? Don't *we* also want to look good? Not good like Fernando, with perfectly coiffed hair and bronzed skin, but "good" on our terms, with the various external symbols and signs of success.

Few of us currently believe that in this day and age we can feel good without looking good. And looking good means looking successful. With a little help from Madison Avenue and *People* magazine, not to mention *The New York Times* Living Section and *Lifestyles of the Rich and Famous,* we got confused. We became utterly convinced that if we were going to project a good self-image, we would have to be reasonably rich; if we were going to be happy, we would have to be very, very successful; if we were going to feel fulfilled, we would have to own lots of good stuff. In short, if we were going to have self-esteem, we were going to have to look as though we had it all.

This Is True for Me . . . Not for the Other Guy

"Look, if Joe down the street is driving an old beat-up Chevy, or eating in cheap restaurants, I don't think any less of him. I know he can be a worthwhile human being. But when it comes to me, I don't feel good about myself if I'm driving that old car. I expect myself to do better than that. It's that simple."

—*Robert, thirty-nine, real estate agent*

"My older sister is also an attorney, and she's very successful and has her own practice. She has this uniform—this grungy old suit, and she couldn't care less about what people think of her. She's smart and terrific and totally sure of herself. Maybe if I was that successful, I wouldn't care either, but I'm in a different world—a corporate world. You have to dress for success, even if you can't afford it.''

—Marnie, thirty-five, lawyer

Among the people we talked to about image, few, if any, were as tough on others as they were on themselves. Both Robert and Marnie understand that image per se is not an accurate reflection of one's self-worth. Yet, in their own lives, they continue to insist upon projecting an image that corresponds to their view of success. And if they are not able to do that, they feel less confident and less secure.

Robert, for example, has recently suffered a serious setback at work. His company is located in an area where there is a real estate slump; his commissions have fallen and he is making far less money than he considers acceptable. He understands that he is not the only one affected by hard times, and that he shouldn't feel ashamed of his financial problems. Yet, he says:

''This is very tough for me to handle. If I have a date, for example, I have to be careful what I spend. No more big spending. This is embarrassing to me. I know it's not just me. I know that everyone is going through some kind of financial adjustment. But that doesn't matter. This is my life, and I should be able to do better.''

It's one thing to get down on yourself because you aren't doing work that you believe is creative, fulfilling, or worthwhile. It's another thing to believe that you are less valid as a human being because you are driving an inferior vehicle or dining in moderately priced restaurants.

What is disturbing about this is how easy it is to become genuinely upset if you believe the image you present to the world is shaky. Whether, like Robert, you are a real estate agent or, like Marnie, an attorney, you probably have very set notions about exactly what your image to the world should be. How big an apartment you "should" have or how expensive your clothes "should" be. Yet so many of us have difficulty achieving our own standards of what should be, that we have to wonder whether or not we are being realistic.

Keeping Up with the Fantasy

We realize that none of us wants to think of ourselves as trying to "keep up with the Joneses." Keeping up with your neighbors is a tired concept from the fifties and sixties. When most of us look around at our neighbors and friends, we see couples who are struggling; we see their financial woes, their stress, their mortgages, and their family problems. We certainly don't want to be like them and we certainly don't want to compete with them. That's too easy.

No, we want to compete with people who have exactly what we want. So what we seem to have done is taken the old "keeping up with the . . ." concept one step further, and in the process made it much tougher for ourselves. Mr. & Mrs. J., the neighbors, have been replaced by Mr. & Mrs. J., the fictional couple we see on television or in the movies. They're who we want to emulate; that's the turf on which we want to compete. And why not?

The people on television live in fully appointed, frequently luxurious apartments and houses—no matter what their income levels. They wear gorgeous clothes; they drive late model cars; they own terrific jewelry. It's the fantasy Jones family, and that's who we want to be like. Even a sitcom such as "Roseanne," while making a sincere attempt to depict a working class family, is guilty of upscaling reality.

Think about it. From an examination of the set, we see that Roseanne's television family resides in a reasonably comfortable house with at least three bedrooms (the master bedroom has its own bath), an eat-in kitchen, laundry room, and a garage. They own a television set, a couple of cars, a microwave, lots of pots and pans, etc. Yet, Roseanne frequently works at the minimum wage, and her husband is often between jobs. Do we all honestly understand that a young underemployed couple with three children is not going to have enough money to live anywhere near as well as Roseanne's television family? Do we all understand that this is a fantasy?

Or do we look at these images on television and assume that everyone else has a more successful life? And, more important, do we then feel embarrassed and ashamed at what we believe to be our own less-than-perfect image?

Hall of Mirrors

"I really want to be involved in a love relationship, but my work involves fine art, and that means something to me. Unfortunately, the only man I've met recently who was at all nice was this doctor who is a Sunday painter. I'm not saying he paints bullfighters on velvet, but his work is just one step removed. It's awful. There is no other reason why I can't develop a relationship with him: he's attractive, intelligent, even well-off. But I can't be seen with somebody who's a rotten artist. It looks terrible for me."

—*Sylvie, forty-two, gallery owner*

When you look at your reflection in the mirror, what do you look for first? Do you look at what you are wearing? Do you look at your face? Do you look at the total picture or do you immediately get detail oriented and start examining yourself for imperfections—a pimple, a piece of lint, stray hairs?

Each of us, when we look in the mirror, looks for something different. That's because we each have a different and unique concept of what it means to have a good image, and what is essential to one person's concept of self may be meaningless to someone else.

Image is crucial to us because, on some level, it is how we define ourselves, to ourselves. Sylvie, the art gallery owner, feels very strongly that she is defined by what she does for a living *and* by the man in her life, and she doesn't want any conflict between them. Another woman may feel that she is defined by her friends. Someone else may feel defined by his address or the size of the apartment in which he lives. For many people, all of these are important, to some degree, in their image construct.

What's interesting, of course, is that even though two people may be in perfect accord in believing that "clothes make the man," they may each have a totally different concept of what it means to be well dressed. One man, for example, may insist upon a tailored Brooks Brothers image; the other may lean toward the Armani look. If you took either of these men, both of whom care about clothing, and put him in the other's "outfit," he would probably feel foolish and out of place. His image wouldn't fit his notion of who he was or who he wanted to be.

It's probably safe to assume that nobody is without image needs. They seem to be an integral part of the human condition. It's one thing to have image needs; it's quite another to be controlled by them. Being controlled by image needs means that you are always a prisoner to a thousand and one external variables that are out of your control and that can keep changing. With this kind of external focus, you'll never be able to achieve any sense of internal peace.

There are two primary ways in which image concerns fuel the dynamics that keep us from having the lives we want. These are:

- *Image cripplers*—all those things that make you give more weight to the way you believe people are perceiving you than the way you are actually feeling.
- *Image fixes*—all those things that give you a false sense of importance, thereby encouraging you to remain stuck in unsatisfactory situations.

What image cripplers and image fixes have in common is that they are both illusory. Neither the cripplers nor the fixes are rooted in reality, but both have the ability to change your mood or other people's perception without changing what is really happening. In fact, they both depend upon illusion for their power.

I Can't Help Worrying about What People Think

Some of the most counterproductive feelings we can have as human beings revolve around a sense of embarrassment or shame because we think we are projecting what we believe to be a negative image. For example, take Aaron, a forty-three-year-old former network executive:

"I'm really upset because I look like a failure. I'm divorced—so my marriage didn't work. Last year I got fired—so my career didn't work. Everyone knows that I didn't get another job. I'm no longer even looking; I'm free-lancing, which is okay, except that it's difficult for me to motivate myself to get through the simple stuff like buying paper clips or stamps and following up on correspondence. I feel foolish standing on line at the post office. I'm too old to be my own messenger. It makes me feel subhuman and humiliated. I look like a jerk."

Two years ago, Aaron was a well-paid television producer with all the expected perks, including a large expense account and a full-time assistant. Although the stress of maintaining his job was giving him migraines and chest pains, it was also giving him access to a multitude of privileges. He says:

"When I was working full-time, I was losing my mind. I couldn't even eat some of those high-priced meals. I would go into the best restaurants in town, and my stomach was gurgling so badly that all I could have was an omelet and toast. It's a fact: I didn't even enjoy all those benefits. And I really didn't like most of the people I was working with. I didn't like the people I was traveling with, and I didn't like the people I was eating with. But I took the *service* for granted. And I took the attitude for granted. People treated me differently because I worked for a major network. When I called people on the phone, they returned my calls right away, because of who I worked for.

"Now, I'm working for me, and I don't have a staff, or anyone, treating me as though I'm important. I actually enjoy working alone; the absence of tension is great. And I'm probably making almost as much money, and I have the promise of more money. But working on a smaller scale—on some level it's demeaning. In my mind, I've become one of those out-of-work guys that people feel sorry for.

"When I run into people I know I find myself lying about what I'm doing. I indicate that I have so much money stashed away I don't need to work. It's all facade. And I need to keep mine intact."

Perhaps nothing is more of an impediment to positive movement that the sensations of shame and embarrassment that Aaron describes. Right now, he acknowledges that he is doing okay financially and that he is feeling much healthier physically. Yet, instead of feeling a justifiable pride that he has managed to become financially solvent and find a new level of independence, he is tormented by an unwarranted perception that he has lost respect among his peers and that people are feeling sorry for him.

Unfortunately, this kind of image concern is all too common among men and women who have built their careers on so-called fast tracks. For them, even though staying on the track may mean experiencing a great deal of pain, they can feel enormous conflict about letting go of the "prestige" that often accompanies such careers.

Success Is Killing Her

Cathleen, who is married to a very successful businessman, is a thirty-six-year-old law partner in an established firm. Originally, her husband was very supportive of her career, but now he honestly believes that his wife's job is destroying her health. Eight years of putting in twelve hour days have taken their toll, and right now Cathleen is suffering from a series of inexplicable physical symptoms that are affecting her ability to function. Although, by her own admission, she is a bundle of nerves, she is unable to stop what she is doing and take control of her life.

Cathleen says that she doesn't stay at her job because she loves the work. To the contrary, she admits that she frequently hates what she is doing. As she explains it, she keeps the job because of how "being a partner" makes her feel. Her role in the organization and with clients gives her a sense of value. The hidden message is that without the job, she wouldn't feel important. She wouldn't feel that she had any real worth as a human being.

She says that when she was very young she "embraced the idea that you could derive your entire identity from your work." And she still feels that if your work is important, you are important. The only problem is that now Cathleen is trapped. If she stops doing important work, to her way of thinking, she stops being an important person—and this is something that she cannot bear.

Cathleen's quest started in high school, when she pushed as hard as she could to get into the best college. While in college, she sacrificed a social life to turn in a stellar performance. Then came law school, a better school, and she found herself even closer to being in over her head. But Cathleen fought and worked and came through with an impressive performance, impressive enough to land her a great starting job with a first-rate law firm and a foot on the fastest track she could find. And then came the seven-year struggle to make partner. She had to run even faster.

And that's how she lives her life, running on the fast track. She is up at five every morning, out the door by six, and she's rarely home before seven-thirty in the evening. She eats dinner with her husband, does paperwork or reads briefs until eleven or twelve, and then crashes only to start again the next morning. She says that she is "frequently too numb with fatigue" to talk to her husband. Even so, she often finds herself volunteering for special projects at the office, or volunteering for committees that make her "look good in the legal community."

Cathleen says that for a while she thrived on the pace of her life, the high energy of her work, but she is now so burned out that she doesn't know what to do. She says that she is ashamed to acknowledge that she can't keep up the pace, and she doesn't see any way to slow down and hold her job.

Cathleen may soon have no choice. Her body is beginning to tell her that she can't keep going. She has developed palpitations, and emotionally she is all raw nerve endings—the slightest provocation is enough to make her scream or cry.

Six months ago, she started having asthma attacks at about four A.M., but they only happened during the week, never on the weekend. She is convinced that it is some form of allergy, even though her doctor has told her that the only thing she is allergic to is stress. Cathleen's husband agrees; he thinks that stress is slowly killing his wife.

Recently Cathleen has started talking about having a baby, not that she actually wants to. Frankly, she doesn't think she would be a very good mother, and, unlike many of her friends, she's never "felt the desire to have a baby." However, Cathleen thinks that having a baby may be a way out of her current nightmare—perhaps the only way.

You see, Cathleen says it would "kill" her to leave her job because of stress. She couldn't live it down; it would feel like a humiliating failure. But no one would ridicule her for leaving to have a baby. Perhaps more accurately, she wouldn't ridicule herself. The loss of importance she feels at work might be offset by the gain in importance she would experience by being a mother.

Cathleen is clearly someone who is unable to accept herself just for being herself. Without a job or a baby, in her mind, she has no real value.

Cathleen and Aaron have both allowed issues of image to dominate their lives. When Aaron was employed, he was miserable and unhappy. Cathleen feels the same way. Yet they both got something from the conditions of their employment. Although their jobs make them miserable, they both received benefits that revolved totally around image. Neither of them has realized how much he or she has given up, in terms of personal happiness, to maintain an "appropriate" image to the outside world.

IMAGE FIXES

"Everything sucks, and you feel rotten about yourself, and then somebody invites you to a really upscale party, and for a few days everything is okay. You know what I mean?"

When your boss is making you feel as though you are expendable, when your friends' successes are making you feel inferior, when you have no social life or when your "significant other" is being rejective—all of these register as blows to your image. And that doesn't feel good. So what do you do? Unfortunately, the common response is to look for something to bolster the image. This is a more expedient solution than examining the core problems that make us feel that way. When we feel bad enough, this need to feel better becomes almost a craving—so we do whatever is necessary to get temporary relief. There are a wide variety of ways in which someone can get "image relief."

For example, somebody who has just been rejected in love suffers an image blow and may immediately go out and find somebody else who makes him or her feel desirable. We have seen that job-related image losses often provoke a similar kind of "quick fix." One woman said that when she lost her high-paying job on Wall Street she responded by going on a spending binge:

"I didn't even think about it. The day I was let go, I felt so terrible, I knew I had to do something. What I did was run up thousands in debt within hours. First I called a limousine to take me home—can you imagine? Then I had the driver stop at all these stores on the way home. I bought dresses, a fur coat, and emerald earrings. As I was doing it, I thought I was being very good to myself because it was taking away part of the edge of being fired. Now I know I was insane. By the next day I came to and realized that not only was I without a paycheck, I had maxed out all my credit cards."

George, a salesman, told us an interesting saga of how his image boost got him into serious debt.

"I remember a couple of years ago, I was feeling really awful about my social life, which was virtually nonexistent. I was living in a new town where I didn't know anybody, and I wasn't having much fun. And I had taken a new job, which didn't have much status. I wasn't feeling good about any of it. Temporarily, I was living in a relative's apartment in a very expensive part of town, and I was surrounded by people with money, all of whom had a lot of flash—gold, Ferraris—that kind of thing. The only women I was meeting were the kind I couldn't afford to date, even if I had wanted to.

"One day I went to a store to get my old watch repaired, and I saw this really extraordinary watch from the forties. It was seven hundred fifty dollars. Expensive, but not expensive like a Cartier. And it was really unusual. I didn't have the money, but I had the money—I could afford it if I was prepared to stretch.

"The salesman started telling me how underpriced it was—how it was a good buy, an investment. It was so striking. I loved the watch. Putting it on just bumped up my whole sense of self. From being just a regular Joe with a Pulsar, all of a sudden, I was wearing this old timepiece. I was a *collector*. This was something I could tell people—women, to be precise.

"So I bought the watch, and within two weeks of buying it, I was back in the store, looking for another watch. After all, if I was going to be a collector, I needed more than one watch. The feeling of walking out of there after each purchase was so great. I remember the rush, the extraordinary high—anticipating, deliberating the purchase, making the buy, going home, looking at the watch. It was a great feeling. Within three weeks, I had three pieces. Within three months, I had thirty pieces.

"Suddenly I was going to auctions, art shows, meeting people, talking about watches wherever I went. I was fantasizing about traveling all over the world, making rare finds. But I was also getting nervous. I didn't have the money for this. And the high didn't last. I had to buy a new watch every week or two to keep me feeling good about my situation. And I couldn't afford it.''

George's obsession with watches is an excellent example of an image fix.

Recognizing Image Fixes

What constitutes a fix differs from person to person, but it always serves the same purpose—it allows you to get through the day, or the week, or any period of time by giving you a temporary good feeling that masks more chronic underlying bad feelings, whether they reflect some type of unhappiness with your work, with the world, or with yourself.

We associate fixes with serious addictions such as alcohol or drugs. Yet, in truth, many of us rely upon different kinds of fixes to which we are equally addicted. Some of them may seem perfectly harmless. Joan, now a successful personnel director, remembers that the most memorable thing about her first job was the fix she got every day.

"I didn't get my first job until the children were all in school—I was almost thirty. As funny as it may seem, what meant the most to me about that job was the coffee wagon. You have to understand, for years breakfast to me was a time of pure chaos. I gulped my instant in a kitchen surrounded by toys, Cheerios, and spilled milk. With the coffee wagon, all I had to do every day was decide what kind of danish I wanted. I would get to work early just so I could take my coffee and the paper and read at my desk. It all felt so clean; I still remember the color of the rug, and the little place I would make for myself at my desk. It was quiet, and I felt like a professional. I looked forward to that feeling I got from the coffee wagon every day. I was able to forget my problems, the bills, the kids, the divorce, the messy house. It was like a fix.''

You can identify a fix in your own life as anything that gives you a high that is not grounded in reality. If you are unhappy with your work, with yourself, or with the world, a fix can soften the situation by giving you a temporary good feeling that manages to mask more chronic underlying bad feelings.

Image fixes can be destructive because they allow for self-deception and rationalization. They can take your mind off your basic problems and create an illusion that some aspects of your life are fine. Fixes don't address the problem; they perpetuate the problem. If your house has termites, for example, and you install some subtle high-tech sonic device that keeps the termites out of sight, you may feel as though you are beating the problem because the problem is not forcing itself into your awareness. But the termites are still eating away at the foundation and your house is still deteriorating.

On an emotional level, a fix will keep you from dealing with the realistic problems that may be gnawing away at your life. Here are some of the more common ''image fixes'' that affect us in our working lives.

Glamour Fixes

Debra, a woman who now works in corporate public relations, remembers when she was working for a firm that was involved in more glitzy endeavors.

"For a fair number of years, I made a huge mistake. I worked for a company where part of the payoff was an opportunity to hang out with people who were rich, glamorous movers and shakers. Although I always complained that I was being used, I guess I thought that eventually I would be a part of that world, be one of them. Let's be truthful: I think I had a fantasy about marrying a rich man. In the meantime, my job was very hard, very time consuming. I was always on call. I ran every time someone needed his hand held, even if that meant getting on a plane in the middle of the night."

Debra says that although everyone envied her exciting lifestyle, she was not being adequately compensated for the amount of work she did and the amount of devotion she gave to her job.

"At first my mother used to call me after I'd been to a party and ask me who was there. She would get a kick out of it. But very quickly her attitude changed. She realized that I was working my fanny off, and not getting money. She kept telling me to quit and find something that paid me enough money. She was really worried about me."

Two elements concerned Debra's mother most: Her daughter was living in a small studio apartment that she couldn't afford to leave; and Debra was not meeting any suitable men.

Debra remembers going to "fancy" parties and coming home afterwards to her studio apartment.

"It was like Cinderella after the ball. The job didn't pay enough for me to afford to buy the necessary clothes, so there I would be in the expensive dress that I couldn't afford, sitting in this tiny place all alone, and I mean alone. Except sometimes the phone would ring in the middle of the night with one crisis or another.

"I worked at that job for four years, and in all that time, I didn't meet one solitary person who I could really date. Oh, guys hit on me, but they were the kind of guys who hit on everybody. One I went out with for a while, but he dumped me for somebody else. Of course I was completely pathetic about it."

In retrospect, Debra views the entire period badly.

"It was all a stupid mistake. It was stupid of me. I didn't concentrate on finding a job that would get me the money I needed. I didn't want to 'compromise' and go work in corporate America. Instead, I expected somebody to give me something. I expected somebody to change my life. It doesn't work that way.

"Eventually I realized what my mother knew all along. Working with people who are rich and successful doesn't make you rich and successful. Working with people who are famous doesn't make you famous. And being able to drop names doesn't make you happy."

Few jobs offer so much opportunity for image fixes as those in the so-called glamour industries. Publishing, art, television, public relations, and film are typically associated with a glamorous life-style. Entry-level jobs in these fields are also notorious for their long hours and low pay. In fact, unless you make it to the very top, these jobs are not as well paid as one might hope; they are also highly competitive and fraught with insecurity. Nonetheless, vast numbers of young men and women, entering the work world for the first time, are often specifically drawn into fields in which glamour is the lure.

Ironically, some of the biggest drawbacks to these glamorous jobs are the blows they can deliver to your image. Unless you get to the very, very top, you are going to be spending a great deal of time with people who, by definition, have more money, more status, more connections, and sometimes even more talent that you do. Therefore, you need an extraordinarily stable sense of self to keep from feeling inferior.

People who are drawn to glamour industries sometimes say they need that sense of "competing against the best" to keep themselves feeling "honed." This is that time-honored conflict between being a big fish in a small pond or a small fish in a big pond. Each has its own set of image boosts and image cripplers.

Expense Accounts—When You Feel Like More Than You Make

Perks such as company expense accounts frequently end up being images fixes. To understand how it works, consider the case of Bob, the ubiquitous middle-management executive, who is being paid $45,000 a year, plus expense account. Just about every day Bob gets to go to lunch at a comfortable restaurant where he can order pretty much what he likes, without carefully considering the prices. About once a month or so, Bob has to go on the road and he stays in comfortable, fully serviced hotels and motels, complete with cable, twenty-four-hour room service, plush carpeting, and concierge.

Bob gets to live like a king while working, eating in good restaurants and staying in good hotels. But when Bob is not traveling, he goes home and eats mashed potatoes. Bob feels so good about himself when he is enjoying his company-sponsored perks that he is able to forget about the inconveniences he suffers while he is "on his own time." After a while, he feels as though the persona he has while entertaining "on the company" is his true self.

Howard, a development exec in the movie business, says that he is fully aware that his expense account has the effect of creating problems in his marriage:

"When my wife and I were first married, we would make dinner together, and it was fun. Now, I have expense-account lunches almost every day. I eat at first-rate restaurants so I sort of feel that I should order something good. In the meantime, my wife is home with the kids eating peanut butter. She still wants to have a grown-up dinner with me. But I'm not that hungry when I have a real lunch, and to be honest, I no longer appreciate our dinners the way I used to. You know, the casseroles, a piece of chicken. It's fine, but it's nothing special.

"My wife is resentful. She says she feels three things: One, she can no longer please me because I'm spoiled. Two, she feels left out—I'm talking about places that we never go to. And three, most important, she doesn't reap any of the benefits from my job. She keeps telling me that this isn't a fair trade-off, and that we would both be a lot happier if I had the money to take home instead of the overpriced lunch."

All of the perks are not found in corporate life. Bill, a former golf pro, says that his perks almost ruined his life because for years they kept him tied to a job that had little opportunity for advancement but lots of opportunity for artificial luxury.

Bill became a golf pro right after college, thinking it was a great temporary way to make a living, see the world, and meet some interesting people. The life-style his new job provided soon became almost addictive.

"My first job was at a posh hotel down South. The job paid next to nothing, but I got a great apartment, all my meals in the hotel restaurants, and use of all the facilities, which were considerable. At twenty-three, I was living like a rich retiree and loving it.

"Finally the day came when I had to think about my future—I didn't want to die a golf pro. So I got a real job, with a company in Philadelphia. Three months later I quit and was back to resort living. I was completely incapable of adjusting to the real world. The perks had poisoned my whole way of thinking. Even going into a restaurant and looking at real prices on a menu was enough to put me into a coma. I wanted my 'staff check.' I remember when I first went to look for an apartment in Philadelphia that I would be walking into these expensive boxes and I would be trying to figure out why I was doing this when I could be living in a gorgeous hotel apartment—with maid service!"

Bill says that he eventually left the resort business, but that he feels as though it took him a full ten years to fully "withdraw" from a world in which he got to live like a millionaire on a pauper's salary.

With just about every occupation, there are a certain number of perks that function as image fixes. Some are there to attract you; others are there to distract you. Companies frequently use perks as a lure to employment, and let's admit it, perks also keep us from focusing on all those things that are less than desirable about our work situation.

Often we don't recognize how emotionally dangerous our image perks are until they are taken away. People who are fired or people who retire are sometimes thrown into shock when they are forced, for the first time, to live without these image fixes. Without realizing it, they have come to believe in the persona they were projecting while on a company expense account. When it's taken away, they don't feel good about themselves unless they are able to replace it with another kind of fix that is at least its equal. Inadvertently, the perk became a fix they counted on.

The Power Trip

A power fix occurs whenever someone feels that he or she is able to control or manipulate others by virtue of superior power and responds by feeling an image boost. If you are the person in the power position, it can become even more heady if you believe that people around you are aware you wield more power than they do, and that they are mightily impressed.

Power means having control. Face it: Everyone hates being powerless and everyone likes being the one to call the shots. For some people, power produces a high that can easily become addictive. These people describe the experience as a thrill, a flash of greatness, a sense of rising above the common man—though usually only for a short period of time. This kind of high can create a distorted sense of one's place in the world. As everyone who has read Tom Wolfe's *Bonfire of the Vanities* knows, the most obvious, and extreme, representation of that feeling is Sherman McCoy's thinking about himself as a "Master of the Universe."

Being associated with money may be the most common way to get a power fix. Money, after all, is the time-honored medium through which people in this country keep score of their accomplishments. It's only natural that being involved with money might make someone feel better about himself or give him a sense of power that is not necessarily reflected in reality.

One young employee on Wall Street told us:

"Of course it's exciting. I'm personally responsible for the movement of millions and millions of dollars, on a daily basis. What I do every day affects the future of small countries! This is the big time."

For some people, just being connected to the financial community is enough to give them an image boost. Arnie, a young trader, said:

"I was attracted to Wall Street because I like being around people who make money. They have a patina, an extra edge that makes them somehow seem stronger, more sure of themselves. It gives you a better sense of yourself just to be near them."

As Arnie discovered, one has to distinguish between making money and being around people who make money. This can be difficult if you are twenty-four, just entering the work world and find yourself, as Arnie did, with a twenty-seven-year-old boss who is making $300,000 a year. The implied message of the contract is that if the twenty-four-year-old does his work, he too will have a shot at the "really big bucks." Arnie, who has since left Wall Street, remembers:

"I would go home and talk to myself about how great I was going to be. I would be thinking things like, Someday that's going to be me. I would think to myself that I was smarter than my boss, had a better education than my boss, and was more stable than my boss. If he could make it, so could I. And this would make me feel terrific about myself. It ameliorated the long hours and the instability. P.S. I was eventually fired, along with my boss."

Big money can bring big power highs, and many people respond to financial windfalls accordingly. One woman we spoke to said that when she flipped her co-op in the mideighties, she felt a sense of power bordering on euphoria. "I was on a cloud. I had made so much money that I was sure that I knew more than anybody else, that I finally had the system wired. It made me intolerable to those around me. Even my family couldn't talk to me. It was pure luck that I made the money, but I was convinced that it was all my doing."

Money isn't the only way to get a power fix. Lawyers, investment bankers, doctors, politicians—professionals such as these wield considerable power by virtue of their occupations. In fact, any job or role that brings with it a certain level of status can provide an image fix associated with power.

The deal makers, such as MBAs, brokers, and lawyers, can sometimes find themselves getting an extra image boost from the thrill of dominating a situation by virtue of superior gamesmanship. While engaged in the deal-making process, you can forget the real down-to-earth problems associated with day-by-day living—at least for a while. For a moment, you can feel pretty great about yourself. Ah, if only that moment could last.

Then, of course, there are those people who derive their sense of power vicariously, by working for others who give the appearance of having power. The trickle-down effect of working for an "important" person can influence one's own image. Jeffrey says his company used to have a CEO whose power trip was matched only by that of his secretary.

"She was amazing. She controlled who the 'big man' saw, who he talked to, who he ate lunch with, and she enjoyed it immensely. In the meantime the CEO encouraged this behavior. I think he enjoyed watching people try to wiggle past her to get his attention. She was a real piece of work. I don't think she had any friends—certainly not at the company. She kept her distance and did her thing, which was to make everyone else miserable.

"Eventually he was shaken from power, and she lost all hers—along with her office. She was completely thrown by it. It was like she didn't know what to do with herself. For a time, she was assigned to somebody else in the company, but she was completely different—it was like watching somebody crumple up in front of you. I'm sure her salary didn't go down, but when she lost that image, she looked as though she lost everything. The change in her was pathetic. Finally she just left—maybe she took an early retirement."

Obviously some people have deep-rooted insecurities that keep them on a continuous search for a sense of power. But it's also important to remember that a visceral craving for power often stems from that existential sense of powerlessness we all share as human beings. Understandably, in a world that none of us can control, we all strive to achieve some level of control over our immediate environment. In reality, there are limits to the amount of control any one of us can truly realize. To use power as a fix further detaches us from ourselves as well as from those around us.

Buying and Spending—The Ultimate Fix

The classic six-room apartment on upper Park Avenue. It sells for 2.4 million and has a moderate maintenance. It has a view, large closets, high ceiling, a full kitchen with marble counter space, and a doorman who remembers your name. Who doesn't want it? And who wouldn't feel better about himself if he could afford to live there?

A Range Rover. It doesn't get many miles to the gallon, but it would look so elegant in the driveway of the summer house. You would feel better about yourself just looking at it and knowing that it was yours, wouldn't you?

And what about that summer house? There it sits, sloped ceilings, skylights, huge windows overlooking the ocean. Can't you just imagine entertaining in that house? Wouldn't you feel great?

Things. Who doesn't want things . . . big things—land, art, horses, cars, furniture, stocks, bonds; small things—clothes, jewelry, cosmetics, equipment, shoes, housewares, and exotic foods. Who hasn't fantasized about owning it all?

Many of us are fully conscious that we use buying and spending as a means of getting an image fix. Gloria, a schoolteacher, says that she is aware of it all the way down the line.

"My most outrageous spending sprees come about because I get a sense of having more money than I do. I get into a store, and I have my little credit card in my hand, and I'm deliberating a purchase. If I had to pay cash, I would walk away, but I look at that salesperson and I know that she knows that I can buy it if I want it. I get off on that. Then, I'm too embarrassed not to follow through because I don't want to lose status in her eyes."

Gloria is very aware that she wants people to view her as somebody who can afford to buy things. She likes that image, and nobody is going to quarrel with the observation that spending money to improve one's image (even when one doesn't have the money to spend) is a common failing.

The Status Fix

"I became a doctor for all the wrong reasons. I had this cockeyed notion of status—you know, within the community. I read this book, I think it was by Vance Packard, when I was in my teens, and it said that doctors had high status within the community. That's what I wanted."

Typically status is derived from being involved in professions that are more established or that require a superior education. At one time, for example, banking carried a great deal of status because only the sons of the wealthy were employed within the industry. The same is true of any occupation that seemed to be connected with an old-boy network.

There are a multitude of ways in which people derive a status fix from their occupations. Just about every profession carries with it a status image of its own. We all recognize that some industries are associated with a higher status than others, and within the specific industries, some companies have more status than others. To the uninitiated, one job in investment banking may look like any other job in investment banking, but those in the know are aware of precisely which firms have the most status.

Status isn't just connected to jobs. For some people, a status fix can be the direct result of owning the right stuff. And conversely, not owning the right stuff is a common way to take away from our feeling of self-worth, a way of crippling our image. Who among us hasn't looked at someone and made an evaluation of the other person's status in the community or the world based upon his or her home, clothing, jewelry, car, or any combination thereof? And who hasn't looked around at his or her own dwelling and possessions and felt devalued because our belongings don't measure up to the ideal?

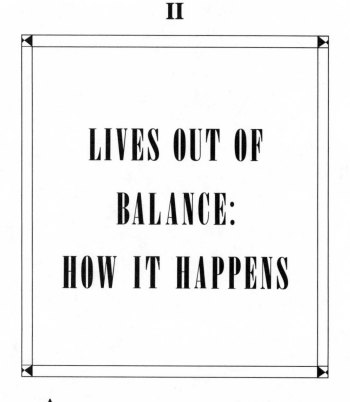

II

LIVES OUT OF BALANCE: HOW IT HAPPENS

All I want to do is put some balance back into my life. I just want to feel as though I have some control again.

—$380,000-A-YEAR TELEVISION EXECUTIVE

5

The Ride of Your Life: Identifying Your Pattern

◤

ARE YOU ON A SLIDE, A TREADMILL, AN ESCALATOR, OR A ROLLER COASTER?

If your life has developed an unmanageable pattern over which you seem to have little control and you sometimes feel as though you are on some sort of a bizarre theme park ride you don't know how to stop, you're in good company. Too many of us feel as though we are "white-knuckling" our way through life. These waking nightmares may not be quite as dramatic as a Schwarzenegger film, but they can still be overwhelming.

Each of us has a different story to tell about the unraveling of our perfect plan, but if you listen to enough stories, you can't help noticing that the underlying patterns and motivations are remarkably similar. You also can't help but see how people's true values and priorities were affected by what happened to them in the workplace. Too often, as things become more and more difficult, people found themselves without genuine satisfaction in work or life. Instead of developing a strong sense of self, more and more often they fell back on issues of image.

What kind of a ride are you on? That depends upon you. Your personality and your style are among the many elements that will determine the ride you are on and the intensity of the experience. Here are the most common:

• *The Downward Slide*—Your life is characterized by a sense of downward mobility, and an inability to reverse this subtle process of erosion.

• *The Never-ending Treadmill*—You feel as though you are carrying the weight of the world on your back and you can't stop even for a moment, without risking its collapse.

• *The Uncontrollable Escalator*—The stakes get higher and higher, the game gets scarier and scarier, and you are up too high to get out without risking a free fall.

• *The Roller Coaster*—New highs and breathtaking falls. Every time you think the ride is about to get comfortable, there is another unexpected twist.

At one point or another over the course of your professional life, you may have experienced all four of these carnival rides—maybe one at a time, or perhaps all four simultaneously. But for most of us, one of these takes over and becomes the dominant theme.

The Downward Slide

Here are the symptoms:

* You are not getting closer to your ideal of a satisfying life, and the light at the end of the tunnel keeps getting dimmer.
* No matter how much effort you have put into your career, you have never been adequately rewarded financially.
* You always assumed you would do better than your parents' generation; instead you need to borrow from your parents.
* You have difficulty affording "normal" social events such as movies and restaurant meals.
* A failure to meet your goals brings with it a sense of shame and feelings of failure.
* You feel as though you were set up by the system.

A downward slide is the sensation most often described by men and women who say that, no matter how hard they work, a sense of stability evades them. They feel they are not doing as well as their parents; they are not doing as well as their peers. They are behind on their expectations; they are behind on their rent.

The major complaints of this group are high expectations and serious disappointments. Typically, when the men and women who talk about being "unable to catch up" entered the workplace, they trusted their own abilities, and they trusted the system. Consequently, they now say that they entered the workplace uninformed; nobody gave them the whole story. Somehow the media, the system, and their own hubris all combined to create some grand deception about the way the world really is.

Michael, a thirty-one-year-old newspaper journalist, is a good example of someone who feels as though he is on a downward slide: "Last weekend I went to visit my parents. They live in your classic suburban raised ranch. Everything matches. To me it used to symbolize everything I wanted to rise above. Now I have a whole different take on it. I realize I will probably never ever be able to afford anything as substantial. I'll never have as comfortable a life-style. I'm clearly a member of the downwardly mobile generation. Right now I have no money, no free time, no security . . . no life."

Michael was the first person we interviewed who used the expression "the downward slide" to describe his life. We interviewed him in a large, noisy Los Angeles restaurant, the kind frequented by young studio executives, up-and-coming agents, minor celebrities, and extraordinarily beautiful women. Michael had suggested the restaurant because he thought it would give us a sense of the current Los Angeles scene. When we arrived, he was standing at the bar, drinking an iced tea, and talking to a glamorous-looking woman in a miniskirt. To a casual observer, it would appear as though Michael is having a good time. In fact, it would appear as though Michael has an enviable, as well as exciting, life-style. But Michael would disagree. He is quick to point out that appearances are deceiving. He says he is profoundly disappointed with how his life is turning out.

"I know what my life looks like, but that's not what it feels like. I guess you could say that my predominant emotion is frustration. All my problems are directly related to how hard I have to work in order to stay alive—the economics of living are doing me in. Each week, I feel I have to give more—in terms of hours, energy, determination, etc. And each week I get less in return for my effort. It's a downward slide with no climbing back up, and I don't know how to change it. That's the frustrating part. I guess by now I expected to have all the things that went with having a good life—a nice house, a nice car, nice kids, etc. Instead I've discovered that there are these humongous trade-offs. It would appear that no one can have an adequate income and an adequate life-style at the same time. For me it feels like an impossible struggle to have any of it.''

Michael, like many members of his generation, puts a great deal of emphasis on goals. He says that everyone he knew set thirty as the magic age by which certain success standards would be met. When he graduated from college, he was no different—he had ''one-year goals, two-year goals, five-year goals.''

By thirty, he expected to have a firmly established career, a reasonable standard of living, a few assets including a decent car and perhaps a small condo, which he would later trade up to a larger place—when he married.

''Up until the time I graduated from college everything went according to plan. I got into a good school, and then I took a year off between my freshman and sophomore years and spent it working in Alaska—a childhood dream of mine. At college, I was an honors student, I was on the debating team, I ran the school newspaper, etc., etc. I was even published in a national magazine.

''Because I've always been so driven, everyone always told me how successful I was going to be. And that's what I expected. More than expected—I just assumed that if I worked hard enough, I would be a huge success and have a good life. My only question was when. The gap between what was assumed and what's happened is ludicrous. When I graduated from college, I was so sure of myself that I purposely took a couple of weeks off because I thought it would be the last time that I would be unemployed. In retrospect that's really funny. Tragic, but funny.''

Michael says that during his last year of college he formed what he thought would be a realistic game plan for his career. His strongest skills had always been creative and literary, but he didn't realistically believe he was talented enough to write the great American novel. What he thought he would do was get an entry-level job in publishing and work his way up through the ranks. He didn't expect to get rich, because he knew publishing was low paying, but he thought he would be successful enough to have a decent life-style. And he thought he would have job satisfaction. With that in mind, he went to the library and did his research.

''I made a master list of all the publishing companies, and in May I started sending out résumés. I put in everything—all the work/study jobs, the writing awards, the fact that I typed sixty words a minute and knew a fair amount about computers. I even enclosed letters of recommendation and some of my publications. I made it clear in my covering letter that I knew I would have to pay my dues and could expect only the most lowly form of assistant or trainee position. By September I was still sending out résumés. I ended up sending out more than four hundred.''

Michael says that during this period he initially believed that it was simply a matter of time before he landed the right job—the job that would get him on a solid career track. As the weeks slid by with no encouragement or positive reinforcement from the outside world, he started to get anxious.

"To earn money, I had taken the world's dumbest job as a chauffeur for a fur company. I would take the president's wife back and forth—that kind of thing. She would be in having her hair done, or at Georgette Klinger's getting her pores cleaned, and I would be racing around looking for an empty phone booth so I could follow up on the résumés and try for an appointment for somebody—anybody—to see me. My favorite story from that job: One day I had to take a courier out to the airport to pick up a shipment of furs. As we pull up to one of these special cargo areas, the courier hands me a *New York* magazine and says to me: 'I want you to take this magazine, an' I want you to put it up on the steering wheel like you're reading it. If anybody tries to hold you up or puts a gun to your head or anything, drop the magazine. That way I'll know not to get back in the car.' "

For Michael this represented more than just an amusing story. For him it felt like a tremendous humiliation because it reminded him of how far removed he had become from what he was expecting.

"Only a few months before this, I was graduating summa cum laude and being told I had a great future, and here I was—at eight ninety-five an hour—being told someone could put a gun to my head. I'm not self-destructive. I don't drink, I don't do drugs. I pride myself on constructive thinking. No way would I normally put myself into this kind of situation. But it was happening. The worse part is that I couldn't quit on the spot. I needed the job."

Michael says that this is the point at which he first realized his brains and his determination weren't enough. He needed more. But he didn't know what that more could be. He says that he established a pattern of second-guessing everything he did. And he found himself becoming more and more insecure.

"I would query everyone I know, trying to understand what was happening. Why wasn't I getting an interview? Why wasn't I getting the job? I would get people to critique me—my résumé, my attitude, my dress. And I listened to everyone, no matter how ill-equipped they themselves were.

"Finally after six months of this I got a job—assistant to an editor in a large company. At first I was thrilled. But the pay was outrageously bad—by any standards!"

Michael says that until he got his first paycheck and took a look at the after-tax total take-home wage, it hadn't occurred to him that he would have trouble covering his basic expenses.

"I had hoped to get a small apartment for myself, but when I started looking, I realized that I couldn't afford a closet, let alone a studio. So I hooked up with some guys I knew. This may sound ridiculous, but after a few weeks of hunting, we counted ourselves lucky when we found a two-bedroom apartment for fifteen hundred dollars a month. There were originally four of us—all tight for cash, but we kept losing the fourth roommate. The original guy left town; the next guy left owing us two months' rent, etc., etc. The last roommate to leave didn't have a job, but he had so much money and such a strange life-style that the rest of us speculated that he was dealing coke. It was nerve wracking—we kept expecting people to show up with guns. Finally we evicted him and decided that the three of us would somehow manage the rent. We used the dining area as the third bedroom and took turns with it. Two months with the privacy of a bedroom and one month having the other guys crawl over you all night long. It all sounds like fun, right? But think about it. This was not three young guys strapped for cash, each paying a hundred or two hundred bucks a month. We were each paying five hundred dollars a month—plus utilities! We were too anxious about money to be having fun.

"The job itself was sort of interesting because you were on the *edge* of an exciting world. People dropped names of famous people who wanted to write books, and editors were always rushing out to lunch. I guess that was part of the payment for the job—the so-called glamour. I saw one celebrity in the reception area, and one day when I answered someone else's phone, it was a minor politician. But that's all the glamour I actually saw. I spent about nine months typing letters, putting books into production, and reading manuscripts. It was hard work, and I put in a lot of hours. At first I was very, very eager. I offered to read manuscripts for everyone; I took work home; I raced around. I brought coffee to my female boss. I did everything I could think of to get ahead. Then I started to look around me. I was surrounded by men and women my age and a little older, and they were all doing the same thing I was. When I asked around, I discovered how few people ever made it off of an assistant's desk."

Michael says he wanted a role model. Someone whom he could look at and know that he or she had made it. But he had none. Instead he was surrounded by people his age, all working as hard as he was, and all complaining because they weren't getting anywhere.

"And the editors didn't seem much better off. They took two-hour lunches, but other than that they seemed to be working all the time. And they complained about working conditions as much as the assistants. It felt to me as if everybody was working hard and nobody was being adequately rewarded.''

While Michael was at this job, there was one major firing, which he says had a tremendous impact on his thinking. A couple of the people he liked most were let go. One of them had been with the company for twenty years. He said this made him realize that he couldn't count on a stable future.

''I had been prepared to work in a relatively low-paying field in return for job satisfaction and job security. It became amazingly apparent that I was unlikely to ever achieve either. I kept borrowing money from my parents who kept telling me that I couldn't afford to work in publishing. You figure it out. I was grossing a little over a thousand dollars a month. I was paying five hundred dollars on rent. And I had to pay taxes and social security, buy clothes, take care of personal expenses, cleaning, etc. And I should add that I had school loans. I would keep all my bills under the bed in a shoe box, pull them out once a month, and try to figure out what to do. What I finally figured was that I didn't have a chance with this occupation.''

Another factor impelling Michael to change direction was the emphasis the media was giving to ''the yuppie.'' Michael says he feels that he was surrounded by people at this point who were totally focused on ''making it,'' and he realized that he too wanted what everybody else wanted.

''This was the Year of the Yuppie. The big joke was that all anyone talked about was the three R's—real estate, restaurants, and roaches. All around me, my peers were scurrying about in their running shoes, trying to look successful, talking about buying co-ops and flipping apartments. I was no different. But I didn't have any money. I couldn't pay my bills, I couldn't ask anybody out on a date, I couldn't do anything. I would read in the paper about the guys only a little older than me cleaning up on Wall Street and in real estate, and I would feel shame and envy. I was barely out of school, and already I could feel myself slipping behind.''

Michael says he became so embarrassed by his financial woes that he felt forced to come up with a new ''game plan.'' He would try to parlay his little bit of experience into a job in either advertising or public relations. Maybe that way he could earn more money.

''My aunt had a friend who had a cousin who owned a market research firm. They hired me to be 'trained' in the back room. That meant sitting around with a bunch of out-of-work actors and actresses tabulating surveys and begging people to let you interview them on the telephone. Everyone assured me that this was 'learning the business' from the ground up. After about six months, it became apparent to me that the actors and actresses had a better chance of getting Broadway leads than I did of getting anywhere.''

So Michael cleaned up his résumé, emphasizing his knowledge of computers, and he got a job with a very, very small firm. There were two people, Michael and his boss, to do everything. Michael answered phones, wrote copy, bought props; he even took a few photographs. He says the clients were the ''saddest lot'' you ever saw.

''But I was gung ho, and I thought I could help my boss, a really nice and really talented guy, get better clients. Within months, he lost his best client, and he went back to working for a large firm. I was out of work.''

However, Michael's boss was grateful for his loyalty and he

gave Michael a glowing recommendation and helped him get his next job at a large high-powered agency.

"This was a *real* job in advertising, with a real company, and real clients. And I had a real title. The job was overwhelmingly tense, demanding, and difficult. Not because of the work—because of the infighting in the company and the tension of trying to keep the clients. I thought I was doing really well. But it turned out that my boss wasn't as thrilled with me as I thought he should be. I honestly think that he was threatened because I became friendly with some of the clients. He started to really ride me in the office, and finally, he called me in one day and told me that my attitude was wrong—I was too high pressured. I thought that's what I was supposed to be! He didn't want to discuss it or give me another chance. It was a killer. I hadn't been making a lot of money, but I had started to pay off some bills and I could see the light at the end of the tunnel. To go back to trying to live on unemployment was too much."

Michael says he was totally discouraged. It was more than two years since he graduated from college, and he was no closer to any of his goals. He wasn't the only one who was upset. He had continued to borrow money from his parents, and they were feeling pinched by his problems. It was their pressure that set him off in a different direction. He applied and was accepted at a graduate school of journalism. This entailed moving back with his parents, taking loans, and the rest. He actually went back to working part-time in the back room of the market research firm.

"I did whatever I had to do to survive, but it was a tough period for me. I still didn't have any money, and I felt too old to be in school again. I felt like a failure. The money thing affected everything—particularly my social life. When I was first in college, I was a star—I had no trouble finding girls to date. But when I was older, not making money, living with my parents—forget it. But school eventually paid off, because I got the degree, and I was able to get a job.''

Michael feels that he was fortunate in not being in a permanent relationship because he was able to take a job anywhere. His first job on a paper down South was a stepping-stone. His assignments got better and better, and eventually he was able to find the job on a larger paper in Los Angeles.

"I'm good at what I do, and I work like a crazy person. So now I finally have a decent job. Some people would even say I have an enviable job. And I love what I do. But I would love it more if I didn't have to do it twelve hours a day. The fact is, however, that I can't slow down. When I look behind me, I see a long line of people waiting for me to slip up so they could have the job.''

As hard as he works, Michael still doesn't think he is doing well. Although his newspaper job is giving him a certain amount of status and prestige, it hasn't resolved his financial problems. That, combined with his heavy work schedule, leaves him with no money and a social life that is virtually nonexistent.

"I know the facts about my life and my prospects for the future. I know my paper isn't *The Washington Post* or *The New York Times*. I know that I don't get the best assignments. I know how much I really make—thirty-five thousand dollars. What can that buy in this economy? For example, I'm driving a nine-year-old car with one hundred thousand miles on it.

"I'm not really making my bills now. I'm always juggling, pushing this aside for that, pushing that aside for this. On the simplest level, I haven't had a vacation in three years. So I'm taking a vacation next week, and I'm thinking, Do I really have enough money to do this? And I know I don't. But I work so hard I feel I should be able to take a week off and go someplace and not think about it without feeling guilty. Suppose I end up having to borrow from my father again? Or I get into more credit card debt—if that's possible.''

Like most of the people we spoke to, Michael complains that he is exhausted from his job, and he has no energy left to expend on anything else.

"Remember also that I've wasted so much time getting on track that I don't think I have a moment left to dedicate to anything that is not career directed.

"Besides, if I take a woman out, I have to think about what it costs. I can't afford to do it regularly, that's for sure. This poverty stuff also affects the way women look at you. If I was a woman I wouldn't want to date someone who has as little chance of making a living as I do. My mother keeps talking about finding a nice woman who will want to struggle along with me, but I think she's living in a time warp—back in the sixties. I've discovered that the women I'm interested in dating want somebody who is a little bit further along than I am. They're already thinking about babies and who is going to pay for the babies' college tuition. The bottom line: I haven't had a long-term relationship in years.

"If I ever get ahead, then I'll be able to think seriously about a woman. Now I have occasional dates with women, most of whom have as little energy left for dating as I do. A couple of months ago I went out with this woman who made her life into an art form. She meditated, she did yoga. She had this whole thing about living. I told her about my schedule, and she told me I was crazy. She's right. I figure I'm going to give this another couple of years. If it doesn't pan out, then . . . who knows?''

Like many others, Michael says that he is becoming frightened at the prospects for his future. He is anxious that his choices aren't going to pay off, and he continues to worry that as he gets older he will slip further and further behind the goals he set for himself.

"I fear that I could turn around in five years and discover that this hasn't really paid off financially in any way, shape, or form. That really scares me. I don't mind work. But the anxiety of never accomplishing anything is something else! It's terrifying to think that my temporary discomfort may not be temporary.

"Unless I win the lottery or there is some kind of miracle, I don't know what's going to happen. All I can hope for is that everybody above me suddenly ups and quits or that somehow I manage to maneuver past them. These are two scenarios that are very unlikely to happen.''

For John and Sarah, losing a job and being unable to replace it is the perfect setup for a sense of being on a downward slide.   That's what happened to John, a thirty-six-year-old computer specialist in Massachusetts. Until his job vanished, John assumed that each year he would continue to get periodic raises and that each year his salary and standard of living would improve. That's why he and his wife, Sarah, felt confident in buying the large comfortable house in the Boston suburbs, and that's why after Sarah had her first child she stopped working.

When she got pregnant for the second time, Sarah decided

that she wasn't going to return to work. Now she is prepared to get a job, but she has been away from the marketplace. The four years she has taken off have set her back. She also worked in the computer industry, where jobs get harder and harder to find every day.

She says:

"For me, it's the stack of bills piling up that has me almost paralyzed. We simply can't pay them. Period. But John is more disturbed by the larger picture—what losing his job symbolizes. He's overwhelmed. You see, in John's head, he was never, ever, supposed to lose his job; that's not the way his world worked."

John's grandfather was a "lifer" with the Metropolitan Insurance Company—almost forty years with them—topped off with the retirement party, the gold watch, and a modest pension. He used to tell John stories about what it was like there as a young man, going door to door collecting insurance premiums from his customers and how he built up a strong, stable client pool over the years that carried him through forty years of service to the company.

Sarah says that right now she could use some of the perks that Metropolitan Life provided for their employees:

"They gave reduced-rate housing. Can you imagine? Really nice apartments! And the insurance, of course. That's how John grew up understanding the working world. You find a company you believe in, and if you like them, and they like you, you stay. And they take care of you, like a family. If you're sick, they're there for you; if there's a crisis, they're there for you. Your closest friends, your social network, your softball game—it all stems from the company. Then when you're sixty-five, you leave with dignity. A party, a pension—

these are the things John took for granted. He would deny it, but I think he grew up thinking his grandfather's life would be his way of life. He grew up believing that, ultimately, he would be rewarded for staying.

"I know this is true because when he took this job, he had other offers, with the possibility of more money. But this one appeared to have stability; everything he said indicated that he was thinking long term, like the rest of his life.

As worried as Sarah is about money right now, she is even more worried about John's mental state. To her, he seems extremely rattled.

"I think part of him still doesn't believe this happened. It's like he's in denial, like he thinks it's only a matter of time before they call him up and give him back his job with a raise to compensate for the inconvenience. He can't handle the possibility of making less money. He's been looking for a job now for almost five months, but no one will pay him anything close to what he was making. We've developed a certain life-style based around what we believed to be a rock-steady income. I'm prepared to cut back, but John is unwilling. He's determined to replace what we had. It's not going to happen."

When John and Sarah felt optimistic about their future, they "splurged" a great deal. Not only did they buy a house, they bought furniture, clothes, equipment. Now they are in the process of selling whatever they can. Last month, they found a buyer for one of their two cars. Sarah says she felt just awful the day they sold it.

"It was like losing a friend. But the bottom line is that we didn't have a choice. I think we don't have a choice about work, either. John is going to have to take a lower-paying job, and I'm going to have to find work doing something— anything. But John isn't at that point yet. He's less willing to compromise. He keeps telling me that I need to have more faith, that I don't understand how important it is never to give up. I disagree—you can only be a cheerleader so long, and I think it's time for me to pack up my pom-poms and start looking for work.''

John acknowledges that he is ''overwhelmingly upset'' by what has happened to his career, but he disagrees with Sarah about what's realistic and what's not. From his vantage point, to settle for a job that pays less than what he was getting would compromise the family life-style to such a degree that it wouldn't be worth it. He says:

''Sarah doesn't really understand. She's the one who isn't being realistic. All this stuff about her getting a job is ridiculous. She can't earn enough. If I stay home with the kids, I can't do the kind of ''looking'' that's necessary, and she can't earn enough to pay for the costs of her working. You know, child care, clothing, transportation—all that stuff adds up. I have the talent and the ability to get and keep a high-paying job, and that's what we need to keep this family afloat. If we settle for less, the house will eventually have to go, and possibly for less than we paid for it.

''The only other possibility, and it's one that Sarah doesn't want to consider, is getting a job somewhere else. Maybe somebody in the Midwest would want me enough to pay for the costs of the move, and we could rent this house until the housing market improved. But Sarah is dead set against moving away from her family—so that option seems to be out of the question, at least for the time being.''

Right now John and Sarah have eliminated as many expenses as possible and are in the process of trimming necessities. Sarah says:

"We were both guilty about spending too much, but I was probably even more extravagant than John—he's always conservative. But in truth we never had enough money for real luxuries like restaurants or vacations. We bought a house. It's not grand; it's just a nice middle class house. And we bought some furniture for the house—beds, a sofa, tables, that kind of stuff. It was enough to put us into a lot of debt. I feel guilty even though I know I shouldn't; these were necessities, not luxuries. But I wish we had the money now when we've had to give up stuff like phone calls, and keeping the heat above 68. We even had a garage sale.

"John has worked so hard on his career. And I've worked too, putting this house together, trying to build a good life for us as a family. Sometimes it feels like it was all for naught. We're so far behind where we started. Even if John got a job tomorrow, we wouldn't be able to pay back our debts for years. In the meantime, every day we get further and further behind."

On the Never-ending Treadmill

Here are the symptoms:

- You are exhausted all the time.
- You realize you have created a "big monthly nut" for yourself, one that will require that you continue to expend the same or more effort on an ongoing basis.
- You believe that you can't slow down without seriously affecting your economic life-style.

- Some days you are so exhausted that you worry you will not be able to continue.
- If you stopped for a minute, something vital wouldn't get done; this is *not* in your head—it's in your schedule.
- Even when you spend time with your family, you are not really able to relate to them, and you are worried that you are shortchanging those you love.
- You don't have the time to introduce a more healthy program—some kind of diet and/or exercise regimen—into your life.

At one time or another, just about everyone has experienced the sensation of living on a treadmill. But for some men and women, the treadmill is never ending, week in, week out, month in, month out, year in, year out. Often those who talk most about the treadmill quality to their existence are those who have pursued the most conservative paths. These are men and women for whom the phrase ''sense of responsibility'' was coined. Their chief complaint: By doing everything they could to insure a secure life, inadvertently they have trapped themselves in a structure that leaves little room for risk taking.

Typically these men and women have professions that required substantial training. As they have gone along through life, they have added levels of responsibility—mates, mortgages, car payments, children, pediatricians, obstetricians, schools, orthodontists, and so on. These people say that once you have progressed past a certain point, it seems as though there is no way off the treadmill, unless one is prepared to write off all his or her training and experience. Most of them also point out that when you have a family, you can't just

change your direction, your earning capacity, and your life-
style without affecting and possibly harming those you love.

**Josh, thirty-six, would like to find a way off of
his treadmill.** No matter how hard Josh works, and he
does work hard, he will always be a good example of the guy
everybody envies. Josh, a partner in a prestigious New York–
based law firm, has all the accoutrements of yuppiedom—the
co-op, the cars, the country place, the high-tech equipment,
the perfectly appointed kitchen with the obligatory goat cheese
in the fridge. He wears Ralph Lauren polo shirts, his wife
wears Laura Ashley skirts, and his baby wears designer jeans.
In fact, nothing in his life doesn't have a label. And he got it
all the traditional way: the right schools, the right jobs, knowing the right connections. But is he happy? And can he stop?

"I don't think I'm trapped on this treadmill forever, but I'm
certainly involved with it right now. Time is a big issue with
me. I never have enough of it. I keep thinking that tomorrow
I'll be able to stop for a minute, but it never happens. The
biggest drawback is that you never know when it's going to
end. It's the old merry-go-round of how much money is
enough money. And it's never enough. Three years ago I
thought, Just a little more . . . Now I'm making twice as
much, and it's still not enough."

Like many others in his situation, Josh feels that his need to
earn is not based on a hunger for money. He stresses that he
doesn't think he is a yuppie and he didn't start out with financial success as his sole goal.

"It's not that I'm greedy. I don't think I am; in fact I need
very little for myself. But what has happened is that, as I've

made more money, I've spent more money. You know, you create a different need for that monthly nut to support your mortgage payments, etc. The apartment costs me five thousand dollars a month. We have a four-hundred-thousand-dollar mortgage and the maintenance is more than a thousand a month. Let me make it clear that this apartment is not a palace. It's an adequate two-bedroom, two-bath apartment in a nice building. It's really not big enough for two children and we want our children to see something besides cement sidewalks. So we have a weekend place at the beach. That costs another three thousand dollars a month. We have two cars. The car that we use to get from place to place, and a jeep that we keep at the beach house. Add in all the costs—parking, insurance, gas, and of course the car payments, and car expenses come to fifteen hundred dollars a month. That's before we start talking about private schools, food, babysitters, health clubs, dental bills, etc.''

In the last year or so, Josh has begun to spend a fair amount of time trying to find a way to somehow alter his life without seriously damaging his earning capacity.

"An issue that I'm always grappling with: Can I, for example, work for a less-demanding law firm and work twenty percent less and take twenty percent less in income? I've actually talked to a couple of firms out of the city. I know I can't go backwards in my firm and do less. You can't go to the other partners, who are also busting their asses, and say, 'I'd like to simplify my life a little bit, so could I work a little less hard.' That's not the way it works. If you're a partner in the kind of law firm I'm in, you're either in there all the way, one hundred percent, or you're out of it. You can't always work twenty-five percent less and make twenty-five percent less. I'm worried that I'll work twenty-five percent less and make seventy-five percent less.''

Yet Josh is aware that much of his pressure is self-generated. He knows that he didn't *have* to make partner in his firm, that perhaps he could have taken a less stressful career path when he was younger. Nonetheless, he likes thinking of himself as someone who can provide for a family, and who can go the extra mile.

''Of course part of the reason I work this hard is ego on my part. Every time I reach another mile, I think, Can I run another one? Can I run a little faster? Can I turn up the incline and see what it's like to do it on a higher level? That's ego. No question about it.''

No matter how much he enjoys being a ''high earner'' he realizes that he can't continue living the way he does.

''It's hard to think about making less money voluntarily. To be honest, it's terrifying. Terrifying! And yet if I don't do that, if I don't make that choice, will I be trapped forever in this life-style where I never get to see my children? Never get to enjoy my life? My wife doesn't work; she stays home with the kids. She takes care of them, not a babysitter. Neither of us believe in this issue of 'quality' time with the kids. I think that's bullshit. It's a rationalization for not spending enough time with your kids. Yet on the other side, it seems that I have decided that it's better, more important, for me to be able to give my kids anything they want rather than be with them more often.''

At thirty-six, Josh has the job he struggled to get, the wife he dreamed of, the children he always wanted. He says he makes more money than he ever imagined he would. Yet he would be the first person to tell you that he has no time to enjoy any of it. Josh is fairly clear on his choices and his conflicts. He says:

"I'm afraid of my own mortality, afraid that there's never going to be enough time left to do what I want to do in life. My father died young so it's a real issue with me, and yet I'm afraid that I can't stop what I'm doing in order to do something else.

"The only time I have with the family is on weekends, but even then I spend much of it apart from them. We drive out Friday night, arrive at ten or so, absolutely exhausted. Saturday morning, we shop for the weekend, bagels and cold cuts and all that shit that you think you might want and never do—so you end up throwing it away or carting it back to the city and throwing it away there. Most of Saturday afternoon I work. I take my portable fax with me, and it's plugged in much of the time. I try to get a swim or something in late Saturday afternoon. Saturday night we all have dinner together. And I take a couple more hours with everybody on Sunday. Then it's time to pile into the car and do the three-hour drive back on Sunday night. It's certainly more relaxing than the city, but I never stop working.

"Living this way makes you weird. You don't have time to think about what you're doing. You don't have time to cut back, or to conserve your financial resources. I had lunch with another lawyer last week who was in a lousy mood. In essence what he said was that he was feeling so shitty, he had to go out and do something for himself, something to justify his terrible life-style. So after lunch, on the way back to the office, he walked into a showroom and bought one of those little BMW convertibles as a present to himself. Just like that. This week I talked to him, and he's in a lousy mood again."

Margaret, thirty-seven, cost accountant and single parent, says that her treadmill goes so fast she's dizzy. We've spoken to many young mothers, married and single, who feel that the "treadmill" best describes their current state.

We met Margaret at a Christmas party she was attending with her two children. Divorced for three years, Margaret has a daughter, seven, and a son, five. Margaret's face is composed, her manner is efficient, her clothes are stylish. In fact everything about her looks "together." It's difficult to believe that she feels as oppressed as she claims.

"I've been working day and night for the last fifteen years. I went straight from college to grad school, straight from grad school to work and marriage. I've never had a day as an adult when I wasn't overwhelmed with responsibilities—from worrying about work to worrying about dinner. A meeting at work, or a meeting with my daughter's teacher, it's all the same to me—just one more thing I have to do before I get to go to sleep. In one way I'm lucky that I never stopped working when my children were born. I didn't have to get back in, and I didn't have to take a salary cut. But on the other hand, I've never had a minute when I could stop and think only about myself, my needs, my feelings, my life."

Margaret says that her day begins at six-thirty in the morning and she goes nonstop until close to midnight. In the morning, she gets breakfast ready, makes lunch for her daughter, gets everybody dressed, walks the dog, drops her daughter off at school, her son off at his babysitters, and drives twenty miles to work.

"If I'm lucky there's not too much traffic or a snowstorm,

and I get there in thirty-five minutes, but on a bad day, it can take an hour. Whenever one of the children is ill, it's a nightmare. My regular babysitter used to be able to cover for me, but then I foolishly got her another job, working for a friend. At first the friend, who doesn't work, told me that she understood that when I had an emergency, I would come first. But a few months ago, my daughter got chicken pox, and when I tried to get my babysitter, my friend had a fit. She told me she was tired of being a second-class citizen and having people take advantage of her just because she stayed home and didn't work.''

Margaret spends so much time talking about her children, it might appear as though they were her only focus, but that is not the case. She has a difficult high-pressure job in a charged atmosphere.

"I don't have an easy job. It's a killer. And I have to be sharp. In my business, mistakes are immediately translated into dollars and cents. I don't really even get time off for lunch—I either eat lunch at my desk, or it's a business lunch. They try to be understanding about my children at work, but I wouldn't try to push that understanding too far. They accept the fact that I can't travel, for example, but if I started showing up late because the kids were sick or something, or looking hassled by parenting problems in the middle of the day, it would not be good for my job.

"In the evening I rarely get home before six-thirty. I'm more fortunate than others because I have a good salary so I can afford some help—not a lot, just some. I have a part-time housekeeper who comes in from four to seven-thirty. She makes a big difference in my life, but she doesn't have time to do any food shopping or laundry or heavy cleaning. What she does do is pick up the kids and start dinner. She stays a little bit later on Wednesdays so I get five minutes to close my eyes and wipe out. That can make all the difference between being okay and being in pain.

"I try to spend extra time with my children every night, have dinner with them, read them stories, watch TV. Friday nights we all go out and do the food shopping and have dinner out. Sometimes the kids opt for a Chinese restaurant. Most of the time, they want Burger King or the local diner. Every other weekend, the children are with their father, so Saturdays I go into the office, and on Sundays I do the laundry, do the cleaning, do the chores, etc., etc. When they're home, I clean on Saturday; Sunday, I try very hard to do something special with them.

"Not only am I totally exhausted, I'm not making it financially. My ex-husband lost his job six months ago, so he's always late with child support. Even when he wasn't, the money was tight.

"I'm so tired most of the time, I'm numb. I've had one bad relationship since my divorce. He wasn't a very giving man, and I really think I only got involved with him because I didn't have the energy to be self-protective. All I could think about was that it was nice to have someone else to do some of the driving. What I hate most is the feeling that I'm missing enjoying the children. I don't want to be tired when I'm with them. I don't seem to be able to give my best efforts to both my job and my children, no matter how hard I try. I can't get away with shortchanging my job, so I think my children are suffering. I have this vision of my children being in a therapist's office twenty years from now complaining that their mother was never available for them.

"I never expected my life to be this hard. It wasn't supposed to be this way. I did everything right: I married my college boyfriend; I developed my career; we waited to have children. The only problem was that we were both so absorbed with our work that by the time we had children we had lost our connection to each other. What little bit of extra energy I had after work, I gave to the kids. The marriage needed feeding and neither one of us had anything left to give to it. The last years, not only was I working hard, I was also always either pregnant or with a young child. We interacted so little, I don't even remember his being around. It's all a haze.

"What are my chances of getting off this treadmill? As hard as I try, I can't think of any logical plan that can change my life. I never used to think this way but now sometimes I find myself hoping I could meet a very rich man who could afford to take care of me and my kids. This is not likely to happen. Oh yes, I've also taken to buying lottery tickets. In the meantime, I keep hoping to make more money so we can go away more, or maybe I can get more help. Anything to make a difference. But right now, I doubt it. My daughter goes to public school, but my son has a learning disability and he's going to need private school. I'm not even sure how much longer my daughter can continue where she is. The school system is falling apart."

On the Roller Coaster

Here are the symptoms:

• Your professional life is characterized by a continual series of highs and lows; one minute you're on top of the world, the next you worry about being out on the street.

• You are driven by a need to make a killing so that you can get out and start a different kind of a life.

• Even though your body is beginning to tell you that it can't keep up with your life-style, you resist changing.

• Regular nine-to-five jobs have little interest for you; you find such an existence dull, mundane, or deadly.

• You handle major setbacks well and tend to recover and surpass previous limits.

• You've always envisioned yourself as someone who would make "real" money.

• You acknowledge that you are a gambler by nature and you like the pressure of a fast track.

At the amusement park, some people race to get seats on the roller coaster. Others wait behind, vowing never, ever, to set foot on one. For these people, just watching the little cars crawling up a steep incline and plunging down the other side is stressful enough.

Those whose day-to-day existence means *living* on a roller coaster are a special and different breed. Often when they start out on their professional careers, they seem to thrive on the very things that most of us would avoid. Roller coaster occupations hold the most appeal for people with more than a touch of gambler in their souls; they are more likely to feel that the spectacular highs are fair compensation for the calamitous descents.

The major complaint of those on a roller coaster is: The spirit is willing, but the flesh is weak. As much as they appreciate the thrills of an up-and-down life-style, the physical toll frequently proves to be too great. Ulcers, migraines, and other stress-related conditions seem to come with the territory.

Some people are naturally volatile, and the roller coaster they live on is one of their own design. But the men and women who describe their work lives as having a roller coaster quality are most often clustered in certain types of professions. Wall Street is the perfect example of a roller coaster environment.

Andy, thirty-two, a Wall Street trader, says his health has been affected by his work.   Andy is a trader for one of the largest and most successful Wall Street firms. When we last interviewed him in late 1991, he said that his earning capacity had still not recovered from the crash of 1987. This, he said, drastically affected his mood.

"Right now my income is holding steady, but it's nowhere near what I had grown accustomed to making. When the volume is down, the work is depressing as hell. I feel fine on the weekend, but when the time comes to show up at the office at nine on Monday morning, my stomach is in a knot. From 1988 through all of 1990, it was agony. I couldn't wait till Friday when everything shut down.

"On Wall Street, you have to develop a gambler's attitude. There are always going to be ups and downs, and you have to be prepared for it. But you don't know how bad it can be until you go through a down cycle. People told me, for instance, that I could make a half million a year, which was true. What nobody told me is that some years you can make thirty thousand dollars. This is also true, and a major problem when it happens. Then you have to realize that there is absolutely no job security here.

"There are no guarantees in this business. This is not like a regular job where you know that if everything goes right you'll earn maybe six percent more each year. However, on Wall Street there is always the chance that when the market turns around, you can make a *lot* of money. So you hang in for those chances. Some people can't take it, financially or emotionally. There are about three hundred brokers where I work, and the turnover rate is about thirty-five percent every year. Nobody lasts that long. Anybody doing this past the age of thirty-five is considered an antique. The depressing part about the work is that you can be very conscientious and a very diligent worker and still be a complete failure at it. I'm considered pretty successful—probably among the top ten percent."

Andy says that during the peak period in the eighties, he made a great deal of money. His job has never been threatened, and he continues to receive offers from other firms, which is a more positive situation than most of his peers have. But he doesn't consider himself a success, as he envisioned success.

"I think many people in my generation thought we would become incredibly successful and wealthy by the time we were thirty. Then we figured we could take it easy, do charitable work, etc. Anyway, it doesn't seem to be working for me.

"I got into this for the money. I thought I could make a lot of money. I started trading when I was still in my teens. I never thought of working anyplace else. I got my first job the day I graduated. Now things are slower. I wouldn't be so fortunate today, but back then it was much more active and I felt a lot more freedom about moving around.

"I was very arrogant back then. You know on Wall Street, you don't get a salary, you get a draw; the first job I took, I didn't like the draw I was getting, and I didn't like the people I was working for so I told them to shove it. I got another job at Company B immediately. I worked there two years, profitable years for them and for me. Then Company C offered me an upfront bonus of more than one hundred thousand dollars to get me to work for them—plus a solid contract. It was irresistible.

"Halfway through the contract, I had some disagreements with the people I worked with. These disagreements involved a lot of lawyers, a lot of money, and a lot of trauma. I was lucky because another company approached me, bought up my contract, and gave me another big chunk of money to go to work for them. That's where I am now."

Andy is so accustomed to dealing with large sums of money that he sounds incredibly blasé about how his work is going. But nonetheless he acknowledges the strain of it and says he finds it very upsetting that he has not amassed a sizeable amount of money. Andy, like so many other single people we spoke to, says that he feels fortunate in not having familial responsibilities.

"The people here who have a wife, kids, and a mortgage someplace in Connecticut are really stewing. If I had bought a house when I had the money, and had a huge mortgage and people depending on me, right now I would probably be jumping out the window. As it is, I still share the apartment I had ten years ago, so my fixed personal overhead is very low.

"Don't let that make you think that I socked away any money. I didn't. I earned middle-range six figures for a few years, but I invested most of it, and some of those investments have not always proved to be very wise.

"Bottom line: Do I have money? No. Do I have debts? Yes. I have about fifty thousand dollars in credit card debt. And I have many other investment expenses. I bought some commercial real estate when I was making money. Right now, it's not paying for itself. I made some other "brilliant" investments. One was supposed to be a tax benefit but then the IRS disallowed all the deductions, retroactively. When that happens, they also hit you with interest and penalties and all the rest. So the bottom line is that I wrote a check for well over one hundred thousand dollars and wrote it off. I just paid the whole thing and walked away from it. It's the easiest way to do this kind of thing. Get involved with lawyers and you get killed with more money. It's not worth it.''

Since real estate was supposed to be a sure thing, not a gamble like the stock market, during one of the good years, Andy bought "five or six" pieces of real estate—for investment only. All the properties are rented. Two break even, the rest are losing money.

"So I'm operating at a real loss every month. I just keep making the payments, extending myself, and figuring that everything has to change—eventually. I guess I spent or invested most of what I made. I went out to dinner a lot.''

As tough and savvy as Andy sounds, he is paying a physical toll for his choice of employment, and he knows he can't continue doing this much longer.

"I'm in my early thirties and I have a ton of medical problems, much of it stress related. I have an ulcer, for example. I actually got the ulcer during a good year—from the stress of working so hard. It comes and goes. I've been hospitalized for it.

"I'm not going to continue this much longer. I'm making plans. Maybe I'll go back to school, get a degree in something simple like social work. I think I might like that.

"Right now I view my life and what I do as a game where

every day there's a winner, and every day there's a loser. I try to stay calm about it all. You have to accept it for what it is: You're always trying to outsmart, outguess, and outperform the next person. Think of it as a giant chess game, on a daily basis. It's all very volatile.''

Mark, twenty-six, Wall Street trader, is still waiting for his big chance.   By the time Mark went to work, the stock market was on the verge of crashing. Consequently, he has never experienced any of the perks that go with good times. Within the last three years, he has held four jobs, tried to start his own business, and been out of work for a total of fourteen months. He is determined to make Wall Street work for him, although it certainly hasn't been easy. He says:

''I've always been very goal oriented, very directed, and I know this is what I want to do. When I was still in school I started working part-time for a very sophisticated money-managing program. These were mostly intern-type things, and they didn't pay very much, but even though I was in school I was working forty, sometimes fifty, hours a week, just to learn.''

Once Mark got his degree, he went to work for a brokerage house that he describes as a terrific place to work. Unfortunately, it went bankrupt within a very short time. Then he was out of work for a few months before getting a job with a company that he says wasn't ''on target'' for his career. At that time Mark had a more traditional attitude toward employment: He wanted to get established with a solid company, one he could plan to be with for a long period of time. So, while he was going through these ups and downs, he continued to search for the ''right'' company.

"I kept trying to get into the training program at what is probably one of the most intensely competitive firms in the financial business in the United States. I kept trying and trying. The fact that I made it to the final culling process is a real feather in my cap. But ultimately it was no go. At first I was devastated, but I didn't let it get to me. I just kept my nose to the grindstone."

Mark's perseverance paid off because he eventually ended up at another equally successful, competitive, and aggressive company. Mark loved working there; he loved the pressure and highly charged atmosphere.

"It epitomized my perception of Wall Street: the gunslinger mentality, very aggressive, very competitive, very, very high paying. I was there about a year and a half. The average week I would say I put in a solid fifty-five or fifty-six hours a week, sometimes more. I was usually at work by seven-fifteen, seven-thirty. Lots of nights I worked until nine. Sometimes it was one A.M. It was intense, but I liked what I was doing there. It was gratifying—deadlines, projects. I was in sales, and we had to maintain a bottom line of profitability. It was high pressure, and I loved it."

As much as Mark loved this job, it ended because the company "purged" his boss and everyone who worked for him.

"We were wiped out. I decided that I could live by my wits so I tried to start my own business. I jumped the gun on it, and I failed. It was five months that were wasted. Nothing worked out.

"Then I got another job, with yet another brokerage house. This one lasted about eight months. I was making okay money—approximately eighty thousand with my bonus. The job was hard but I didn't have to kill myself. I don't want to go through again what I just went through where I worked twelve hours a day on stupid projects and ultimately got fired for my efforts. It's just a waste of my time. I was there about eight months before the company did an across-the-board lay-off. I've been out of work now about three months, but I think I'm going to get this job that I interviewed for last week.''

Mark is very aware that his life-style has not been good for his physical or emotional well-being. He has been drinking far too much. And then there is the ulcer that he got during his first year on Wall Street.

''The ulcer comes and goes depending on the pressure. I look at it as a trade-off for what I do. In this business, there are a couple of things that happen to you. For one, your hair thins— because you tend to pull at it. When things get tense you find yourself doing all these quirky nervous little things, like pulling at your hair, biting your fingernails, pulling at your moustache, if you have one, to cope with the stress. You have to expect to buy a lot of Maalox. I chug it. It's part of my daily ritual.

''I started drinking more heavily a couple of years ago. There's a lot of drinking among the people I know. It's interesting—not only did I start drinking more, I started drink-ing with a goal in mind. It was an avenue to purge myself— sort of my daily bilge pump. Most nights after work, I would go to some sort of social situation, and I would drink to ex-cess. I don't particularly like the taste of alcohol, and I don't need it as an outlet—that's not what I'm about. I think the best explanation is that when I'm working everything I do is in-tense, including my drinking. When I was working all those hours, that's when I drank the most.''

Mark feels he is fortunate because when he worked, he was earning a good salary, and he didn't get into heavy debt. He says that his experiences have altered his attitude toward making money.

"I don't have savings, but I don't have any debt. I've kept my overhead low. I was sharing a big place with five other people, which was incredibly chaotic. Now I have a small studio on my own. The people one rung above me, particularly those with families, they're having problems. They are making enough to make the house payments, but the car is about to be repossessed—that kind of thing. You have to be smart and not get stuck in that kind of bind. I think I can do it. I really do. Most of the people I know here are making just enough money to get their toes wet and see what it could feel like to make the real money. And they are working very hard.

"I think I've always had the same goal. I'd like to use up half of my life to make a couple of hundred million bucks and then spend the second half of my life giving it out charitably. That would make me happy. But I can see that it's not as easy as I thought it would be to make the real money. But if you're aggressive enough, you can probably do it. I think I'm aggressive enough."

As aggressive as Mark may be, he admits that he is beginning to experience some conflict about his career choice.

"The last time I was unemployed, I had what you could call an existential depression. Nothing was working out—my love life was bad, my work life was bad. It all got to be too much and I started thinking about all the things I wanted to do and enjoyed doing. I love the country. I grew up in the mountains, and a large part of me would like to escape out West. Right after college, when I couldn't find a job, I started a small landscaping business. That's something I really enjoyed. No hassle. But when I think about doing that sort of thing, I worry that it's running away. And I don't think it's mentally healthy to avoid problems. But I was happy doing what I wanted to do every day, not what somebody else told me to do. So much of what I've done at work is a waste of time.

"My biggest work disappointment? That I'm not further ahead. That I spent all those hours working with people that I'd be happy if I never saw again. That I can't maximize my creativity. That I'm going against my grain and forcing myself to be shaped in a manner that I don't think is me.

The Uncontrollable Escalator

Here are the symptoms:

• Although you have achieved an acceptable level of success, you can't stop.
• You continue to up the ante in your life, even though you recognize the self-destructive nature of your behavior.
• The financial structure of your life is so complicated that you couldn't even begin to explain it to another human being.
• You have never, not even for a moment, reached a point where you felt materially comfortable—no matter how much you have.
• You have absolutely no life outside of your work.
• You are totally leveraged.

What's it like to spend one's life riding on an uncontrollable escalator? It's a tense, frightening experience. Like the roller coaster, it has all the heart-stopping anxiety of waiting for the moment when it will all peak, and the ride will start down. But for some inexplicable reason, an uncontrollable escalator doesn't peak. It just keeps climbing, and as it does, the pressure escalates. The work load escalates, the responsibilities escalate, the debts escalate, and the stakes escalate. If you are on an escalator, your overriding sense is that you can never get off, and you can never stop moving, because if you do, the ride will be over. And there will be nowhere for you to go but down, down, down.

Possibly the most driven of any group, the men and women who live on escalators are usually entrepreneurial types. Determined to get to the top, frequently they are also determined to do it for themselves.

Their biggest complaint: They can't stop working and worrying long enough to enjoy any of their accomplishments. Escalator personalities frequently say that their possessions own them, rather than the other way around.

Suzanne, a real estate developer in Colorado, describes herself as the ''Queen of Leverage.''

At any given moment Suzanne holds title to a dozen real estate properties. Some of them she has bought with the hope of selling them immediately. Others she is managing herself as rental properties, keeping them for the long haul, or until the market changes. As fast as she sells one piece of real estate, she buys another. Because the market is ''soft'' right now, Suzanne is also trying to start another business.

Suzanne, an elegant-looking woman with a quick sense of humor, lives in a beautiful large home decorated with impressive antique Navajo rugs. But Suzanne rarely, if ever, gets to enjoy her environment because her life is all work and no play. Six nights a week she works till close to ten P.M., and on her one day off she is busy researching other businesses that might afford her a slightly less anxiety-filled existence.

Spending a day with Suzanne is like spending a day with an emergency room surgeon. Few conversations are completed without being disrupted at least once by the intrusive sound of her beeper. She runs from her home phone to her car phone to various pay phones along her routes, forever complaining about no-shows, weekenders, interior decorators, and, of course, the sad state of the current real estate market. Still, you can't help feeling that if anyone is making real estate deals it's Suzanne. Her language jumps back and forth between friendly conversation and industry jargon. Her inexhaustible supply of energy and unfailing enthusiasm is impressive; it's hard to believe that in spite of her command of the business, Suzanne is struggling and frightened. She says:

"It was very easy creating this monster, but the maintenance is killing me. I created all this shit. I bought the rugs, I bought the real estate. But it gets to the point where everything you own owns you. That's where I am."

Suzanne is such a born entrepreneur that it's difficult to believe that less than twenty years ago she was a poorly paid schoolteacher in a low income neighborhood.

"When the twins were little, and I first got divorced, I went on peace marches and lived in subsidized housing. I had three part-time jobs and grants and loans to go to school. I had absolutely no money. With it all, something told me to create equity. I borrowed from friends, I deprived myself of necessities, I used student loans to play the stock market, and I did good. In short, I did whatever I had to do to raise enough cash to put a down payment on this rundown little house. I spent all my spare time renovating it and that's how I started. I was lucky because housing around Aspen doubled and tripled. By the time it was ready to sell, it was worth a lot more than I paid. So suddenly I had equity. I used my equity to start buying more real estate.''

Suzanne emphasizes that at first real estate was just a hobby and she had no intention of doing it for a living.

"When I got out of school, I went straight to work as a special ed teacher in an alternative school system. I was a total do-gooder, but I kept playing with real estate. Every spare penny I had, I invested. I kept selling, and reinvesting my profits on better buildings. It worked fine until the government started cutting back on social programs, and I found myself unemployed. I wanted to get a job in the private sector, but my résumé had ''bleeding heart liberal' written all over it, and I didn't have the right experience. I couldn't find a job doing anything. The only other thing I really knew was real estate, so I took the course, got my license, and I've been doing real estate ever since.''

Suzanne says that she is so deeply in debt that she can't even count everything she owes. She leverages everything. At the moment, she has seventeen credit cards, which she juggles.

"I've always lived in debt. Doesn't everyone? When you live this way, what happens is that your credit gets better and better so you can borrow more and more. I created my dream using credit cards, financial aid, and the subsidies that were available in the seventies. Right now, I have a lot of property. But what people don't realize is that there is a big difference between profit and cash flow. Cash flow is cash flow. Profit is profit. The story of my life is that I buy real estate, and I sell real estate, and I don't have any money to speak of. It's all credit, but if somebody tried to collect on it right now, it would be all over. When I was poor, I never thought that I would reach a point where my life would revolve around what the prime rate is, but that's what's happened.''

When the real estate market is down, as it has been recently, Suzanne is under even more strain than usual.

''I should move to someplace smaller, but I can't sell my personal residence because paying all those taxes would kill me. I'd lose equity and lose cash. I can't sell the other stuff because I don't have the cash to take the loss.''

Suzanne says that her real problem right now is that she doesn't know how to keep what she has without spending more than she has.

''I don't know how to stop adding on without backsliding and having less. I have to spend money to make money, and with this economy, my overhead keeps getting bigger. I still have the car lease. I still have the car phone. I still have advertising. I still have expenses in my buildings—boilers break, water leaks, people don't always pay their rent. People move out. Everything takes money. When I don't have it, I get very nervous.''

Since Suzanne is totally self-made, she has a very visceral sense of what it means to be without. She says she got ''hurt'' in the stock market crash of 1987, and she got scared.

''It's easier going up than it is going down. I don't want to go down. I've done it both ways. I had never been poor until I was poor, and I don't ever want to be poor again. It's a cliché, but it's true—the minute you have something, you have something to lose; the more you have, the more you have to lose, and the harder you have to work to keep it.''

Suzanne, who says that she rarely sleeps more than four hours a night, complains that she's never able to rest, never able to stop. She says that there are not enough hours in the day to do everything she has to do.

"Essentially I run three businesses so I work a lot. I come home eleven, twelve at night, all charged up. The adrenaline's flowing—who is going to sleep? I have to keep thinking up new stuff, so my mind is going constantly. Also it's gotten much more competitive. Anybody who can't make it any place else comes west and gets a real estate license. What keeps me going is looking for a solution.

"My personal life? It's a joke. It's totally sacrificed. That's how it has to be. If you want it to work, you have to put your whole focus on it. It's consuming. My beautiful home is a place to visit. I'm never there. I'm a juggler, and I'm a survivor—I don't drink. I don't do drugs. I work.

"When I started out, my dream was kind of to be where I am. But I didn't know that I couldn't just sit back and enjoy it when I got there. It's like you never get there. They keep moving the carrot. It's on a stick and they keep moving it. As soon as you get the game down and you think you've got it together, they change the rules, damn it. They rewrite the tax laws, or something, and you've got to do some more to make it fit. I can't see how I can ever stop working. And I don't want to work anymore. I'm totally frustrated. I'm tired. Give me a break.

"I guess with it all, I do think that I am successful because I do keep achieving the goals I set. But my goals keep getting higher. Each new achievement is a new high so I keep looking higher. It's somewhat like an addiction."

* * *

Michael, John, and Sarah on the slide; Josh and Margaret on the treadmill; Andy and Mark on the roller coaster; Suzanne on the escalator—what do they all have in common? They are all giving everything they've got and still not getting what they hoped for. All of them sacrificed a balanced life. Now they want to change that.

III

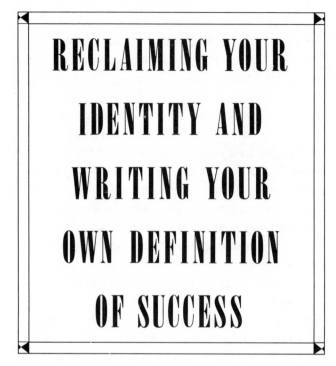

RECLAIMING YOUR IDENTITY AND WRITING YOUR OWN DEFINITION OF SUCCESS

It sounds like a cliché, but it's true—in many ways getting fired was the best thing that ever happened to me. I used to complain endlessly, to anyone who would listen. I would go on about how dreary my personal life was. I would talk about balance. But the way I was leading my life, there was no room for a social life, there were no empty spaces for me, or for other people, and there was absolutely no balance.

The first couple of months without a job were terrible. I didn't know what to do with myself, and many of the people I worked with didn't have time for me once I wasn't part of the official "network."

149

These were people that I was accustomed to spending a lot of time with. Discovering that they weren't really friends was very painful and a terrible blow to my ego. But I made other friends, I got back in touch with people I hadn't seen in ages, and I started working on my relationships in general.

I view those first three months when I was unemployed as a recuperation period. I felt as though I was recovering from an illness—you know, getting strength back slowly. Strength to be a human being again, to notice things and to stop thinking only about the latest deal, what your boss was up to—all the office intrigue stuff that passes for a real life.

Eventually I had to downscale in terms of a job. I moved to another city where it was less expensive, and I had more value. In most ways these changes have been wonderful for me. Of course I'm scared, but I'm doing things. I got myself a cute little apartment; it's not as glamorous as the one I used to have, but I like it just as much. It's interesting—in a new town, where I didn't have to worry about the people I already knew thinking any less of me, I found it easier to economize on rent. I joined a couple of clubs, I have dates, I go to the gym. On weekends I make myself get out—I ride my bike, I go to the park—and I find that I meet people. My social life has definitely improved. Even though I'm making less money, and I still owe a ton, I'm getting my debts in order. All in all, life feels much better.

—CAITLIN, FORTY-THREE, HOTEL ADMINISTRATOR

6

Dealing with Your Feelings/Dealing with Your Facts

◧

THE COURAGE TO CHANGE

If you want to change your life for the better, you have to be prepared to change yourself for the better. But there's a problem: Few of us adapt well to change; change creates stress even when it's good change. That's one of the reasons why serious change takes serious courage. Change is so scary that most of us don't even know how to approach it realistically.

When people think about changing their lives, they often think only in terms of grand dramatic gestures. They dream of becoming sheep farmers in Australia, or escaping to the Rockies to write the great American novel. Thinking like this can effectively destroy your ability to make constructive changes in your life; change on this scale is more than frightening, it's next to impossible. If you are a responsible, albeit burned-out, forty-two-year-old surgeon with a spouse and three children, you may have thoughts about heading for Tahiti, but it is not likely that you are going to ever be able to leave your family, your practice, your tennis partner, or your pet schnauzer. You don't have to head off for the South Seas with a paintbrush in your hand in order to have a better life. If you are unhappy, you can change the way you feel without replacing all the components that comprise your way of life. All you have to do is stop putting off the inevitable and start doing the personal work that is necessary to make your life more manageable.

STARTING OVER WITHOUT STARTING FROM SCRATCH

"I don't really want a different profession—I just want to be more successful at the one I have. I don't want a different wife—I want to get along better with the one I have. I don't want a vastly different life—I just want less anxiety and more time to enjoy the one I have."

—*Curtis, forty-one, statistical analyst*

Curtis realizes that just because his particular expectations have not been fulfilled as precisely as he had hoped, that doesn't mean that he should write off his genuine accomplishments or diminish the skills he has acquired. He doesn't want to take bold drastic actions; he just wants to feel more comfortable. When we think about it, most of us probably would agree with Curtis. While there are certainly days when anyone feels that he would prefer permanently to chuck it all and head for the Amazon, or Paris, or Timbuktu, most of us recognize the farfetched quality of our more extreme career daydreams.

In fact, few among us would be able to sustain more than a week or two of watching the flock munching on a meadow, and even fewer have the talent or discipline necessary to write in a lonely cabin, with the local moose population providing the only diversion. There is usually a reason why we chose the work we did, have the friends we do, and lead the lives we lead. If you are like most people, you don't want a different life; you just want to be able to manage the one you have. You don't want a different career; you just want to feel successful in the one you've chosen. It's true that most of us are in conflict about our problems. We want our lives to improve and we want to feel good about ourselves, but we don't want to have to create a whole new self. We want to rock the boat a little, but don't want to rock the boat too much.

What about you? Do you need to create a whole new life plan, or do you just need to alter your attitudes or to make a few minor adjustments in the way you live? Whichever, the first thing you need to do is come to an honest acceptance of the fact that there is a real problem and it has to be addressed.

IF YOU WANT TO FEEL GOOD, YOU HAVE TO BE WILLING TO LOOK AT WHAT MAKES YOU FEEL BAD

It's very painful to look at your picture of the way the world works and realize that it has serious flaws. It's equally painful to stare at your reflection in the mirror and admit that your method of living in the world isn't working and that you can no longer continue to ''give yourself six more months,'' or another year, or two, or five. You have to acknowledge that a new phase is being thrust on you, whether you like it or not. You have to do some hard thinking *now*. Before you can solve the problem, you have to look at the problem.

We hesitate to use the word *denial* here because it tends to evoke images of deeply troubled men and women who are unable to face their problems. Most of us career-oriented types don't think of ourselves that way. In fact, we see ourselves as being particularly able to face problems head-on. Nevertheless, denial is the operative word here.

For example, many of us are deeply disappointed because we haven't reached our goals. Disappointment is a tough emotion to deal with because it also contains an element of shame. You know, all that old ''I guess I'm not really a winner; I feel ashamed'' stuff. Instead of dealing with the feelings these thoughts bring up, most of us just deny that the problem exists. We maintain face to the outside world and we rationalize to ourselves. For example:

- Barbara says that she doesn't care that she hasn't had a promotion in three years, but she has a shopping habit that will not quit.
- Richard says his high-pressure job is great, but he gets drunk three nights out of every five.
- Seth says he thrives on the high-pressure atmosphere of being a litigation specialist, but he has an ulcer that keeps returning.

These people are all in denial. Barbara refuses to connect her spending habits with her disappointment; Richard says that with his kind of job, "drinking comes with the territory"; Robert refuses to acknowledge that his ulcer is his body's way of telling him that something is drastically wrong. This type of thinking indicates that they are not dealing realistically with their situations. This is what denial is all about.

Since it's a mechanism that keeps the pain away from consciousness so that we're not always unhappy, denial can sometimes be very self-protective. If we are in denial, we are refusing to look at something because it's way too painful; but not looking at it doesn't make it go away. Remember, denial doesn't change anything. More often than not, refusing to look at our problems honestly contributes to the feeling of being stuck. Until we stop avoiding, we can't find solutions. Frequently, what we are trying hardest to avoid is the way we feel.

SHAME, EMBARRASSMENT, HUMILIATION, AND OTHER FEELINGS TOO AWFUL TO MENTION

If you are like most people, you have feelings you don't want to face, attitudes you don't want to change, and parts of your personal history that you don't want to examine. Typically, the second we start to look closely at what's going wrong in our lives—at what we have done in the past and what we are doing in the present—we find ourselves caught up in a maelstrom of emotions that are not pleasant. We usually find ourselves experiencing wave after wave of feelings that make us uncomfortable. We get embarrassed and begin to worry about how we look to others. We start to squirm and hide the facts, sometimes even from ourselves. We don't know how to take the emotional risks that may be necessary in order to establish new patterns. We don't know how to deal with our mistakes, with our economic problems, or with our disappointments. In short, we feel humiliated or embarrassed or ashamed.

Within the last few years a great deal has been written about the toxic effects of shame. Many of us are aware of the groundbreaking work done by John Bradshaw. Nonetheless many men and women fail to recognize when shame is at work in their own lives. To them shame is seen only in severely dysfunctional families and associated with problems such as alcoholism, drug abuse, or child abuse. They don't recognize the ways in which feelings such as shame can be cripplers in their own lives.

For instance:

• Nancy, thirty-four, is the typical single parent. She is overstressed, overworked, overburdened. She is ashamed that she doesn't have enough money to live up to the American dream. Many of her friends are very comfortable. She worries that, as a single parent, they see her as a "needy case." She would like to be a glamorous divorced woman living the kind of life she sees depicted on the TV, but that's not the reality she faces. She is a good mother to her daughter, Melanie—some people might say "too good." Nancy disagrees. She knows that she spoils Melanie in some ways, but feels she deprives her in others. For instance, Nancy believes she doesn't spend enough time with Melanie; she has never adequately dealt with how her divorce affected her daughter; she is often so tired that she rages at the child. She is guilty about all of this and tries to compensate by making certain that Melanie, eleven, is not deprived on a material level. For example, every summer Melanie attends a camp that costs more money than Nancy can afford, and every year Nancy puts herself into a terrible bind trying to pay for this camp. To Nancy, not being able to send Melanie to camp would be overwhelmingly shameful.

Nancy has levels of shame. She is ashamed of the failed marriage, she is ashamed that people will discover that her relationship with Melanie is sometimes stormy, she is ashamed to be seen as part of a group (single parents) who are more economically needy than others, she is ashamed that she hasn't married again, and she is ashamed and embarrassed that others may feel sorry for either her or her daughter.

• Paul, an Ivy League MBA, does not make as much money as some of the people he went to school with, but he, unlike others he knows, still has a job. Several years ago, he and his wife bought a Victorian house. He expected a financial miracle to take place. It hasn't. Paul is deeply ashamed and embarrassed by his financial woes. He expected that he would be doing better. His wife, who knows the facts about the family finances, is as unrealistic as her husband. For a wide variety of reasons, she doesn't want to put their sons into day care and go back to work. When Paul tries to talk to her and explain the strain he is under supporting all of them, he finds it impossible because she doesn't want to hear what he has to say. She keeps repeating the same thing, "Something will happen—maybe we'll win the lottery." So Paul backs off. In the meantime, he is working harder and harder and getting more and more into credit card debt. It is easier for him to do this than it would be to force his wife to realize that either she goes back to work or they have to move. His wife also has her problems with shame. It's very important for her to feel that she has the respect of her family. In her mind, if she goes back to work, her family will know the truth: Her husband doesn't make enough money to support them adequately. She is certain that they will think less of him, and her. She doesn't want that to happen.

• Debbie and Leila are both attorneys for the same firm. Debbie has married a legal aid attorney who has no rich relatives. Her friend Leila has married a rich accountant with a whole family full of rich relatives. When Debbie and Leila get together socially now, Debbie can't keep up financially. She is ashamed of this; sometimes she is even ashamed of her husband, whom she loves very much. Debbie knows this is stupid. She didn't think money mattered to her; that's why she joined legal aid. But she can't stop herself. It was one thing when she didn't make much money as a single woman; as a part of a couple, she thought she would have more because "people expect more from a couple." She looks at her apartment, and she looks at Leila's house. She looks at her furniture, and she looks at Leila's furniture. She looks at her clothes, and she looks at Leila's clothes. Debbie doesn't really care about the money, but she is ashamed that she and her husband seem to have so little.

• Dick has worked for the same law firm for the last eight years. He did not make partner. He is deeply ashamed, and doesn't know what to say to his friends. He likes his job. The pay is okay. Since he can't face the shame he feels, he is thinking about leaving, which he doesn't really want to do. For Dick it will be easier to tell everyone that he was dissatisfied. In that way the whole issue of why he didn't make partner will be covered up. By now Dick has almost convinced himself that he really is dissatisfied and should move on.

As outsiders looking at their situations, we can see that it's foolish for Nancy to feel ashamed that she has less money than her contemporaries. Nancy needs to work on developing a better way of communicating her love for her daughter; she needs to foster the kind of mother/daughter relationship that puts more emphasis on family and less on spending.

It doesn't take much insight to realize that Paul is beating himself up unnecessarily. His anxiety is ruining his health and his feelings of well-being. Without shame or embarrassment, he needs to accept the fact that he is not going to be able to make his mortgage payments without help. He and his wife need to introduce more honesty into their communication. They have to get over their feelings of embarrassment and reassess their expectations of each other. Either she will have to go to work, or they will have to move.

Debbie is interesting because not only is she ashamed that she and her husband are not well-off, she is ashamed that she is ashamed. She has always espoused attitudes and values that are the opposite of what she is feeling. She can't talk to anyone about what she is feeling. It is making her confused and angry. She needs to examine her feelings and resolve her conflict before it affects her marriage.

Dick doesn't like to think about his situation very much; it makes him too unhappy. He needs to evaluate why he is so worried about others. If he is happy in his job, and he feels adequately compensated, why is he concerned that he will not look as successful as some of his peers?

When you read all these stories you will see that there is a common theme. Nancy, Paul, Debbie, and Dick all are deeply concerned with how they look to others. They worry that they may not look rich enough, or successful enough, or happy enough. They worry that others may recognize the pain in their situation and thus feel sorry for them. They worry that their disappointments may show and they will look foolish and pathetic. All of these concerns are directly related to their need to feel that they appear to be "okay" and that people will approve of who they are and what they are doing. In many instances people are more worried about how they look than how they really are.

LIFE ISN'T ALWAYS PERFECT, AND YOU'RE NOT ALWAYS PERFECT EITHER

Look around you and you can't help noticing that there is a great deal of chaos, confusion, and disappointment. Just about everyone is having some kind of problem. If you're having economic problems, you're not alone. If you're having housing or real estate problems, you're not alone. If you're having personal problems, you're not alone. If you're having tax problems, you're not alone. If you're having career problems, you're not alone. If you are scared of the present, you are not alone. If you're terrified about the future, you're not alone.

These are difficult times, and our personal difficulties reflect what is going on in the world. So why is it that when you look at another person's problems you are able to understand all that, but when you look at your own, you blame yourself? Why do you think that you should have had the ability to foresee the future? When you look at someone else's choices, you can see why they made perfect sense at the time they were made. But, when you look at your own, why are you so aware of the ways in which your judgment was flawed? Why are you inflicting standards on yourself that you're not inflicting on others?

And most important, why do your problems and "failure" embarrass you so much? Are you feeling a sense of shame because your family doesn't own as much as the Ewings or get along as well as the Huxtables? What are you trying to prove and to whom are you trying to prove it? Do you ever wonder why you are so deeply affected by what others think or why you struggle so hard to gain the approval of others?

PARALYZED BY THE NEED FOR APPROVAL

Society is fixated on approval. We take it so much for granted that you can hardly pick up a newspaper without seeing another poll that rates how much approval the public is giving to our leaders or their policies. Presidents, congressional leaders, governors, and mayors all pay close attention to their approval ratings, but politicians are not the only ones hungry for approval. We all want to be accepted and liked. In fact, sometimes it seems as though there is no greater need than the need for approval, whether it be the approval of our parents, the approval of our peers, or the approval of society in general. And what better way to get approval than to make such a mark with our careers that even our harshest critics must yield to our success?

Huge chunks of our lives are devoted to getting approval, and it goes without saying that at times we have all done things as much for approval as for our own self-fulfillment. The line between the two is often sufficiently blurred that we have a hard time keeping it straight in our own heads. Gaining approval can make us feel so good that we can become convinced that we have made certain decisions primarily for our own satisfaction. We think the voice of approval or disapproval is our own, but in reality it is more likely to be the internalization of the voices we heard in our childhood.

Needing approval is not necessarily a bad thing. It only causes problems when your own sense of value relies so much on someone else's opinion that it controls much of your behavior. This is a very fragile way to live in the world. It colors all your choices and affects all your decision making. If your craving for approval is great enough, you will never be able to stop because there will always be another person to please and another mountain to climb.

For most of us, it's difficult to envision a world in which we would receive unconditional approval and acceptance. For a minute, try to imagine what that would be like. Think about how that would make you feel. What would you do differently? What would be exactly the same?

For a moment, let's pretend that the only person you have to worry about pleasing is yourself. And nobody can judge you. Nobody but you is going to know how much money you make, what you do for a living, how many bills you have, where you live, what you own. Nobody but you is going to evaluate your disappointments or your achievements.

A PERSONAL INVENTORY— TAKING AN OBJECTIVE LOOK AT YOURSELF, FOR YOURSELF

"I can't write down how much money I owe or figure out who I owe it to. It's too depressing."

—Frank, thirty-eight

Everyone can understand how Frank feels. If you owe money, facing exactly how much you owe may feel overwhelming. If everything in your life isn't going the way you want it to, spending time thinking about it can make you feel even more uncomfortable. Nonetheless, when you are serious about change you have to figure out your debts and you have to come to terms with your reality. This kind of examination is essential. The only way we can make informed choices is to inventory our lives, figuring out what we did right or wrong in the past, and what is keeping us stuck in the present. That's how we can decide what we want in the future. With that in mind, let's put down on a piece of paper some of the facts about your life.

The following personal inventory is to help you evaluate what is causing you stress—and distress. It was designed to help you look at some of the issues that you may have been avoiding. Answering these questions may prove to be difficult, or even depressing. All of this is to be expected. Remember what we know about denial—when something is painful or causes unhappiness, there is an almost automatic tendency to push it away and try to bury it. Evaluating your reality may well challenge your denial system, and this can generate anxiety. But we all know that we can't move forward unless we face our facts.

We think it's important that you actually try to write down your answers so that you can confront and evaluate what you're doing, or not doing, in black and white. If you're going to find balance, you have to come to terms with the things that are creating a lack of balance. Writing everything down will give you an honest appraisal of where you stand in life right now. So get a pad and pencil and begin.

1. When you embarked on your current career path, what kind of "payoff" did you expect to receive?

   Rank in order of importance, with 1 signifying the most important, those things that you expected to receive from your work life. If you had no expectations in regard to a particular item, indicate so with a 0. (It's okay to assign the same ranking to more than one item.)

a. Status among your friends   _____

b. Status within your industry or
    profession   _____

c. Self-esteem   _____

d. Job satisfaction   _____

e. Sense of self-worth   _____

f. Status within your family   _____

g. Financial success   _____

h. Fame   _____

i. Security (medical plan, pension, etc.) _____

j. Free time to do other things   _____

k. Social opportunities (dates, friends,
    etc.)   _____

l. Interesting life-style   _____

m. Making a contribution to society   _____

n. Glamorous life-style   _____

o. Other (specify)   _____

2. Which of these "payoffs" has your career actually pro-
    vided?

    Rate on a scale of 0–10 (10 being the highest), the level
    of satisfaction (S) you've received in each of the follow-
    ing categories. (If it applies, give the same rating to more
    than one item.)

                                          (S)
                                         (0–10)

a. Status among your friends   _____

b. Status within your industry or
    profession   _____

c. Self-esteem   _____

d. Job satisfaction   _____

e. Sense of self-worth   _____

f. Status within your family   _____

g. Financial success   _____

h. Fame   _____

i. Security (medical plan, pension, etc.)   _____

j. Free time to do other things   _____

k. Social opportunities (dates, friends, etc.)   _____

l. Interesting life-style   _____

m. Making a contribution to society   _____

n. Glamorous life-style   _____

o. Other (specify)   _____

3. In which of these areas have you been disappointed in the amount of "payoff" you've received?

   Rate on a scale of 0–10 (10 being the highest), the level of disappointment (D) you've received in each of the following categories. (It's okay to give the same rating to more than one item.)

                        (D)
                      (0–10)

   a. Status among your friends   _____

   b. Status within your industry or profession   _____

   c. Self-esteem   _____

   d. Job satisfaction   _____

   e. Sense of self-worth   _____

   f. Status within your family   _____

   g. Financial success   _____

   h. Fame   _____

    i. Security (medical plan, pension, etc.) _____

    j. Free time to do other things   _____

    k. Social opportunities (dates, friends, etc.) _____

    l. Interesting life-style   _____

   m. Making a contribution to society   _____

    n. Glamorous life-style   _____

    o. Other (specify)   _____

4. What is your single biggest disappointment and why?

   _____

   _____

5. Do you ever feel that "the payoff" you are trying to achieve keeps receding and is always just a little bit out of reach?

         Yes_____   No_____

6. If yes, how often do you feel that way?
Some of the time _____Most of the time _____All of the time_____

7. Do you share these feelings with family or friends?

         Yes_____   No_____

8. If not, why not?

   _____

   _____

9. How hard do you think you work?
    Very hard_____   Moderately hard_____
         Not hard at all_____

10. Are you currently working harder than you want to be working?

         Yes_____   No_____

11. How many hours a week do you spend at your workplace?
    _____

12. How many additional hours do you devote to work at home?_____

13. How many additional hours a week do you find yourself preoccupied with thoughts about your career and/or your work?_____

14. When you started out, how hard did you envision working?
    Less hard_____   Harder_____   About the same
    _____

15. If you feel you are now working too hard, in the beginning did you anticipate a time when you would be able to cut down on your work load without significantly affecting your income? Yes_____   No_____
    When did you think that would be? Year_____

16. Right now, do you think that there is a time in the realistic future when you will be able to cut down on your work load without significantly affecting your income?
    Yes _____   No_____
    When do you think that will be? Year_____

17. Have you, in the last two or three years, purposely cut back on the number of hours you spend working?
    Yes _____   No_____
    Did it affect your earning capacity? Yes__   No__

18. Do you consider yourself a workaholic?
    Yes _____   No_____

19. Do the following people in your life consider you a workaholic? Check any who do.
    a. Your spouse   _____

b. Your children _____

c. Your romantic partner _____

d. Your close friends _____

e. Your siblings _____

f. Your mother _____

g. Your father _____

h. Your coworkers _____

i. Your business partner _____

j. Your employer _____

k. Other (specify)_____

20. How much do you enjoy your work?
A great deal_____   Some_____
Very little_____   Not at all_____

21. Do you ever find that you have to give yourself pep talks to keep going? Yes_____   No_____

22. What kind of things are you telling yourself?_____
_____
_____
_____

23. Are all the hours you spend working absolutely essential?
Yes_____   No_____

24. Are all the work-related social events you attend absolutely essential?
Yes_____   No_____

25. Are all the work-related meetings you attend absolutely essential?
Yes_____   No_____

26. How many hours a week do you think you could cut back without seriously affecting your productivity or your earning capacity?_____

27. Do you ever find yourself attending business meetings/dinners/lunches/breakfasts just to fill time or look busy?

     Yes_____   No_____

28. Do you ever find yourself attending business meetings/dinners/lunches/breakfasts in order to fulfill an image or "look the part"?

     Yes_____   No_____

29. Do you find that you sometimes get a "high" from being overwhelmingly busy?

     Yes_____   No_____

30. Do you ever get a letdown or "lost" feeling when the work pressure eases and you have a block of unstructured time?

     Yes_____   No_____

31. What in your life is most important to you?
    Rank in order of importance, with 1 signifying the most important, the parts of your life that have the most meaning to you. (It's okay to assign the same ranking to more than one item.)
    a. Your social life   _____
    b. Your family life   _____
    c. Your own creative work   _____
    d. Your career goals   _____
    e. Your sex life   _____
    f. Your leisure time   _____
    g. Your hobbies (sports, reading, etc.)   _____
    h. Your spiritual life   _____

    i. Your mental and emotional health   _____

    j. Your physical well-being   _____

    k. Your personal development   _____

    l. Your intellectual development   _____

    m. Your political beliefs   _____

    n. Your social causes   _____

32. Who is important to you? Rank in order of importance, with 1 signifying the most important, which relationships in your life have the most meaning to you. (It's okay to assign the same ranking to more than one item.)

    a. Your spouse   _____

    b. Your children   _____

    c. Your romantic partner   _____

    d. Your friends   _____

    e. Your siblings   _____

    f. Your parents (one or both)   _____

    g. Your employer   _____

    h. Your coworkers   _____

    i. Your business partner   _____

    j. Your clients or patients   _____

    k. Your pets   _____

    l. Other (specify)   _____

33. Have the various components of your life benefited (B) or suffered (S) from the way you deal with your professional path?

	(B)	(S)
a. Your social life	_____	_____
b. Your family life	_____	_____
c. Your own creative work	_____	_____

d. Your career goals　　＿＿＿＿＿　　＿＿＿＿＿
e. Your sex life　　＿＿＿＿＿　　＿＿＿＿＿
f. Your leisure time　　＿＿＿＿＿　　＿＿＿＿＿
g. Your hobbies (sports,
   reading, etc.)　　＿＿＿＿＿　　＿＿＿＿＿
h. Your spiritual life　　＿＿＿＿＿　　＿＿＿＿＿
i. Your mental and
   emotional health　　＿＿＿＿＿　　＿＿＿＿＿
j. Your physical well-being　＿＿＿＿＿　＿＿＿＿＿
k. Your personal develop-
   ment　　＿＿＿＿＿　　＿＿＿＿＿
l. Your intellectual development　　＿＿＿＿＿　　＿＿＿＿＿
m. Your political beliefs　　＿＿＿＿＿　　＿＿＿＿＿
n. Your social causes　　＿＿＿＿＿　　＿＿＿＿＿

34. Have the relationships in your life benefited (B) or suf-
    fered (S) from your work habits or career goals?

                                    (B)　　　　(S)
a. Your spouse　　＿＿＿＿＿　　＿＿＿＿＿
b. Your children　　＿＿＿＿＿　　＿＿＿＿＿
c. Your romantic partner　　＿＿＿＿＿　　＿＿＿＿＿
d. Your friends　　＿＿＿＿＿　　＿＿＿＿＿
e. Your siblings　　＿＿＿＿＿　　＿＿＿＿＿
f. Your parents (one or both) ＿＿＿＿＿　　＿＿＿＿＿
g. Your employer　　＿＿＿＿＿　　＿＿＿＿＿
h. Your coworkers　　＿＿＿＿＿　　＿＿＿＿＿
i. Your business partner　　＿＿＿＿＿　　＿＿＿＿＿
j. Your clients or patients　＿＿＿＿＿　　＿＿＿＿＿
k. Your pets　　＿＿＿＿＿　　＿＿＿＿＿

35. On a scale of 1–10 with 10 being the highest, how would you rank the amount of pressure you feel each day?_____

36. What factors contribute most to the pressure you feel? Rank in order of importance with 1 being the highest rank.
    a. Demanding profession _____
    b. Demanding employer _____
    c. Personal ambition _____
    d. Financial pressures _____
    e. Family pressures _____
    f. Job insecurity _____
    g. Competition in the workplace _____
    h. Insufficient time _____
    i. Physical problems _____
    j. Personal problems _____
    k. Social problems _____
    l. Romantic problems _____

37. Do you ever wake up with the sensation that "I can't keep doing what I'm doing"?
    Yes_____ No_____

38. Do parts of your life seem unmanageable?
    Yes_____ No_____

39. Right now, what are the most unmanageable elements in your life? Elaborate as extensively as possible on each one that you circle. (Use a separate piece of paper.)
    a. Financial responsibilities
    b. Family responsibilities
    c. Work load

    d. Personal obligations
    e. Parental responsibilities
    f. Housework
    g. Debt
    h. Alcohol dependency
    i. Drug dependency
    j. Gambling
    k. Social life
    l. Romantic life
    m. Other (specify)_____

40. Is money, or the absence of it, causing you a great deal of anxiety?
Yes_____ No_____

41. Do you worry about your financial future?
Yes _____ No_____

42. Are you making more or less money than you anticipated making at this point in your life?
More _____ Less _____
Same as anticipated_____

43. Do you feel that no matter how much money you make, it never seems to be enough?
Yes _____ No_____

44. Do you feel that no matter how much money you are making, you still can't relax and feel secure?
Yes _____ No_____

45. Do you think most of the people you know also worry about money? Yes_____ No_____

46. Compared to you, do you think they worry about money more_____? Less_____? The same_____?

47. If you could point to the factors most responsible for your current economic problems, what would they be? Rank in order of importance with 1 signifying the greatest importance.
    a. Low-paying profession _____
    b. Substandard salary or income _____
    c. Excessive spending _____
    d. Taxes _____
    e. Real estate market _____
    f. Children's expenses _____
    g. Spouse's expenses _____
    h. Inadequate training or education _____
    i. Keeping up with the Joneses _____
    j. State of the economy _____
    k. Fewer opportunities _____
    l. Additional expenses from being a single parent _____
    m. Credit card debt _____
    n. Other (specify) _____

48. Do you feel you were given inaccurate information in terms of what you could achieve financially?

    Yes_____   No_____

49. Where did you get this information? Check any that apply.
    a. Peers _____
    b. Teachers _____
    c. Family _____
    d. Media _____
    e. Other (specify) _____

50. Many people have been negatively affected by the ups and downs of the real estate market. Are you one of them? Yes_____ No_____ If so, how? Check any that apply.
    a. Mortgage payments too high   _____
    b. Rental payments too high   _____
    c. Can't afford to move to larger space   _____
    d. Can't sell in current market   _____
    e. Can't afford to buy   _____
    f. Can't afford different quarters   _____
    g. Other (specify)   _____

51. Have you made any questionable investments in the last five years? Yes_____ No_____ If so:
    What motivated you?_____
    What made the investment bad or foolish?_____
    _____
    Do you feel you were overly optimistic when you made the investment?_____
    Do you feel you were the victim of a hard sell?_____
    Were you responding to outside influences such as newspaper or television stories?_____

52. Are you in credit card debt? Yes_____ No_____
    If so, how severe? Very _____ Moderately_____
       Minimally_____

53. Every year, is your debt increasing? _____
       Decreasing? _____ Staying the same?_____

54. How much do you owe?_____

55. Do you have a precise list of whom you owe, how much you owe, and how much interest you are paying?
                   Yes_____   No_____

56. If not, why not?_____

    _____

    _____

    _____

57. Realistically evaluate your financial needs and expectations.

    How much money per year do you need to make ends meet?_____

    How much money do you need to make you comfortable?

    _____

    How much money do you need to make you feel secure?

    _____

    How much money do you need to make you feel happy?

    _____

58. In what ways do you think you are unnecessarily extravagant? Check any that apply.

    a. Restaurants   _____
    b. Clothing   _____
    c. Furnishings   _____
    d. Travel   _____
    e. Unnecessary purchases   _____
    f. Taxis   _____
    g. Services (housecleaning, laundry, etc.)   _____
    h. Other (specify)   _____

59. Are you too tired to economize? Yes _____ No_____
    If so, on which of the following do you spend a great deal of money? Check any that apply.

    a. Household help   _____
    b. Labor-saving appliances   _____
    c. Preprepared foods   _____

d. Dry cleaning and laundry service   _____
e. Personal assistants   _____
f. Restaurants   _____
g. Taxis, car service   _____
h. Gardener   _____
i. Plumber, electrician, etc. for jobs
   you could do   _____
j. Private schools   _____
k. Summer camps   _____
l. Other (specify)   _____

60. Do your work habits ever make you feel so deprived and miserable that you go out and spent money just to make yourself feel better?

Yes_____   No_____

61. List the things you spend money on to make yourself feel better.

_____
_____
_____
_____
_____

62. What is the biggest financial mistake you have ever made?

_____

Why did you make it?_____

_____

Why is it a mistake?_____

_____

63. What in your emotional makeup do you think makes you particularly vulnerable to certain kinds of financial "mistakes"?_____

64. What concrete steps can you take to make sure that you don't make the same kinds of mistakes again?_____

65. Realistically, how much money do you think you have "wasted" in the last year? _____What was it spent on?

66. When you take an honest look at your financial difficulties, what percentage of the problem do you think is caused by the economy in general? _____Your behavior or choices?_____ Other reasons?_____

67. Are your economic difficulties affecting your self-esteem? Yes _____ No _____If so, in what way? _____

68. Are your economic difficulties affecting your relationships with others? Yes _____ No _____If so, in what way? _____

69. Do you think you can be absolutely honest about your financial situation with the following people? What are the reasons why you can or cannot be honest? (Use additional paper.)

	(Yes)	(No)	(Why?)
a. Spouse	_____	_____	_____
b. Parents	_____	_____	_____
c. Siblings	_____	_____	_____
d. Best friends	_____	_____	_____
e. Coworkers	_____	_____	_____
f. Mentors	_____	_____	_____
g. Children	_____	_____	_____
h. Neighbors	_____	_____	_____

    i. Other (specify) _____   _____   _____

70. Do you have any self-destructive behavior patterns that you feel are linked to your work demands?

    Yes _____   No_____

    If yes, what are they? Check any that apply.

    a. Drinking   _____
    b. Recreational drugs   _____
    c. Compulsive spending or shopping   _____
    d. Overeating   _____
    e. Oversleeping   _____
    f. Destructive personal relationships   _____
    g. Other (specify)   _____

71. Have you taken any positive steps to deal with any of these behaviors, such as becoming involved with a twelve-step program or seeing a therapist?

    Yes _____   No_____

    If not, what is keeping you from getting outside help?__

    _____

72. Are you experiencing any of the following? Check any that apply.

    a. Headaches   _____
    b. Anxiety attacks   _____
    c. Blues (mild depression)   _____
    d. Stomachaches   _____
    e. Irritable bowel syndrome   _____
    f. Temper outbursts   _____
    g. Crying jags   _____
    h. Insomnia   _____
    i. Backaches   _____

    j. Significant depression   _____

    k. Other (specify)   _____

73. If you answered yes to any of the above, are you now seeing a physician for treatment or diagnosis?
    Yes _____   No_____

74. Are you taking "good care" of yourself in terms of getting regular medical checkups, dental checkups, etc.?
    Yes _____   No_____

75. If not, why not?_____

_____

76. Are you now, or have you in the last five years, regularly taken any of the following? Check any that apply.
    a. Prescription ulcer or stomach medications
       (Zantac, Tagamet, Pepcid, etc.)   _____
    b. Nonprescription stomach medications
       (Mylanta, Maalox, etc.)   _____
    c. Antianxiety medications   _____
    d. Antidepressants   _____

77. Do you feel that your need for any of the above drugs was in any way work related? Yes _____   No_____

78. In the last five years have you experienced any substantial weight gain or loss that you feel is connected to job-related stress? Yes _____   No_____

79. Do you have any job-related anxiety lasting longer than a few days? Yes _____   No _____If so, what are you doing about it?_____

_____

80. Do you feel that you have balance in your life?
    Yes _____   No_____

If not, what are the elements that are lacking?_____

_____

How much time do you set aside each week for personal recreation?_____

How much time each week do your devote to your personal relationships?_____

How much time do you spend each week furthering your intellectual interests?_____

How much time each week do you set aside for your own spiritual growth?_____

As you think about your answers to this exercise, it's essential that you remember that this is not a test. There are no right or wrong answers. These questions are meant only to help you gain insight into your behavior. If you don't like some of your answers, don't start judging yourself. You are only doing this for yourself, to help you get it straight in your head what is making you unhappy, and what is making you happy. The goal is greater understanding into what you are doing. This is the first step in helping you find balance and get your life moving in a more positive direction.

7

Getting Honest

◪

EVERYONE ALWAYS TALKS ABOUT GETTING HONEST, BUT what does it really mean? Getting honest with yourself means being able to look at *all* parts of yourself—the parts you like, the parts you can't stand, the parts you understand, the parts you can't fathom, the parts you accept, the parts you would prefer to forget, the parts that scare you, and the parts that make you feel as though you are the sanest person in the universe.

Getting honest means understanding that you will try to disguise and conceal elements of your personality that don't jibe with the image you wish to project to the world. Getting honest means struggling through these feelings, knowing that you won't always be happy with what you're discovering, but recognizing that the final outcome is worth it. Ultimately it means acceptance of who you are right now.

If segments of your life aren't working, it's essential to recognize when you are part of the system that created the problems. Odds are that before you can change your external environment, you will first have to change parts of your internal environment. Sometimes you may need to change the way you think. More often, you are probably so confused that you don't know what you think. Unless you figure out what you think and why you think it, you are not going to be able to affect the system or change the way you interact with the world. Unless you are clear about what you value and what is truly important to you, you are not going to be able to lead your life in a way that reflects these values.

This means that you are going to have to force yourself to evaluate your situation honestly. This isn't easy for anyone. We all lead lives that are filled with people and complications and a thousand and one factors, each of which influences the way we behave. All of these complications, in turn, tend to give every one of us a thousand and one excuses and rationalizations for behaving the way we do.

If you want to change your life, you have to make the leap and get past all of these excuses and rationalizations. You have to get honest with yourself. You have to start thinking clearly even if you can't immediately start behaving differently.

LOOKING AT YOUR CORE ISSUES

Getting Honest about How Much Ego You Have Invested in Your Choices

"Of course I'm unhappy with what I'm doing, but I have ten years invested in this. I'm not going to change now."
—*Jack, thirty-two, commodities broker*

Everyone is always very aware of how much time and energy he or she has put into a particular life plan. For most of us, it's more than time and energy that we have invested. We also have enormous ego investments in being the way we are. Sometimes that's what we can't let go of, no matter how unhappy we feel.

Let's say, for example, that when you were nineteen years old and a sophomore in college, you decided that you wanted to be a lawyer. You started out by talking to your advisors, who reinforced your ego by telling you that you were smart enough to get into a good law school; you informed all your friends and family, who, for the most part, thought it was a terrific decision. Friends began reinforcing your sense of self-worth by telling you how much money you were going to make. So you hit the books, confident that you had the brains to make a good law school, worried about the LSATs, and fantasized about your future on the Supreme Court and your snappy BMW.

Now, fifteen years later, you are a thirty-four-year-old burned-out attorney. It doesn't matter whether you made partner or didn't. It doesn't matter whether you took the high road of public service, or the financial promise of the private sector. You are weary and worn. You would like to do something to change the way you feel about your life. But what are you going to do? You have made all your financial decisions based on being a lawyer—a lawyer, for example, should own real estate so you bought real estate. Your clothing reflects your profession, your car reflects your profession, and your friends reflect your profession. Sometimes you feel that your status within your family is dependent upon your status in the legal community. For years you have even impressed dates as well as chosen dates primarily on the basis of what you do for a living. In short, you look, act, and think like a lawyer.

Even though you are completely fed up with your life, so much of your ego and so much of your identity is invested in being a lawyer that you don't even know how to think of yourself in any other way. And you're not sure you want to think of yourself in any other way. That would mean turning your back on all those years, all that work, all that toil, and all that pain.

You're not even sure what it is that's making you unhappy. Maybe it's not being a lawyer, maybe it's your specific firm or work environment. Maybe it's the work pressure. Or do you love the work and hate the hours? Is it the cases? Is it the people? Is it your love life—maybe everything would feel better if your personal life were more stable?

How do you begin to think about this? How do you begin to separate all the conflicting emotions, needs, and advice? What's important? What isn't? Can you really give up the expense account, the important-sounding title, the big apartment? Should you? Could you? Should you move? Should you stay? What would people think if you changed your career? Your life? What would you think?

This sort of examination can be frightening. You have so much invested in your choices that you realize you can't question them without threatening your ego. So much of our identity is wrapped up in everything we have done up to now, so much of our sense of self, that it's brutally tough for all of us to get honest about our ego involvement. Yet, time and time again, people who have made serious changes in their lives tell us that unless we are clear about where our sense of self, our identity, is coming from, we will never feel free enough to be comfortable with change. This is true whether the changes are ones we choose or ones that are forced upon us. Here are some questions to ask yourself:

• Are you more worried about what people might think if you lose your job than you are about actually losing your job?

• Are you overly concerned about having to admit to yourself, and others, that some of your choices were wrong?

• Do you find yourself unable to change any of the elements of your life without worrying that you will be wiping out everything that you have struggled to accomplish?

• Do you feel that you would jeopardize your sense of self if you made a significant change in your career track, your standard of living, your place of residence, your job title?

• Do you feel that your identity is so wrapped up in what you do for a living that you are terrified about any changes?

• Do you believe that any job loss or downward career moves will automatically mark you as a failure?

As you consider your answers to these questions, think about how deep your fears and other feelings go. If your ego and your sense of identity somehow got overly tied up with your career, you may be emotionally vulnerable to the natural ups and downs that many careers take. We all need to learn to lead our lives in a way that a strong sense of self is maintained independently of any specific life choices we might make. We're not saying this is easy, but it should be part of the way each of us thinks about our personal development.

Getting Honest about Your Image Fixes

None of us enjoy a sense of self so intact that we are completely immune to the "highs" that are attached to image fixes. But sometimes it's difficult to understand why image fixes can be so destructive. In fact, for the typical overworked and overstressed person trying to get ahead, it may feel as though those occasional fixes are the only pleasurable moments. After all, what's so bad about enjoying glamour, power, or status? The answer is that when you are dependent on fixes for pleasure, you are involved with illusion. Consequently, you are not able to find realistic solutions for those situations that may be causing problems in your life.

Living in an addictive society means that any one of us can get "hooked" on something. Instead of being hooked on a substance, you're hooked on a process. This is what is called a process addiction, and we see this as another kind of "fix." Being hooked on status, for example, may not seem as destructive as being hooked on drugs or alcohol, but in many ways, a process addiction such as this will serve the same function. These fixes tend to confuse thinking and actively restrict constructive change. Process addictions will make it easier to deny the root causes of your unhappiness.

Getting honest about your image fixes will help you clarify some of the complicated issues in your life. This kind of honesty will shine a light on where you're getting stuck and why you're getting stuck. Image fixes also sometimes play a crucial role in our choices. Our need for them jumbles our thinking and confuses the real issues. All of this requires serious examination.

For all of us, there are people and situations in our lives that can give us real pleasure, but there are also those situations that give us just enough of an artificial high to keep us hooked into nonproductive life patterns. Learning to make distinctions between these two categories will give you a starting point to begin changing your life.

HOW TO RECOGNIZE THE
IMAGE FIXES IN YOUR LIFE

Everyone has certain areas in which he or she may be most susceptible to an image fix. Looking over the following material may help you decide which ones apply to you.

Are you vulnerable to power fixes?

1. Do you ever find yourself thinking about how your own power makes other people feel?

2. Are you comfortable with a sense that you are controlling someone else's behavior? How does that make you feel?

3. Does your work role cause you to look down somewhat at others?

4. Does the thought of clinching a huge deal make you feel like you are truly one of the chosen?

5. Do you enjoy having others treat you as though you are an authority figure?

6. Does your role at work give you a sense of self-importance?

7. Do you enjoy feeling as though you are more important than the people around you?

8. Are you highly competitive and do you enjoy defeating others?

9. Do you actually find yourself spending a lot of time thinking about power?

10. Have you ever made a choice in your life that was motivated by power and had it come back to haunt you?

Are you vulnerable to glamour fixes?

1. Do you fantasize about having a more glamorous life?

2. Do you like to think of yourself as leading a more glamorous life than other people you know?

3. Do you think you would be a lot happier if only you were part of the "right" crowd?

4. Do you get a thrill from dropping the names of exciting people you've met?

5. Do you live for the chance to go to important events?

6. Are you overly forgiving of people who have charisma?

7. Do you sometimes find yourself judging people based on who they are, or who they know, not on what kind of people they are?
8. Are you very aware of the "right" clothes, the "right" restaurants, the "right" social events?
9. Do you truly enjoy the company of the glamorous people you know, or do you get a special thrill just from being around them?
10. Do you dread the notion of being seen as just another "normal" person?
11. Have you ever made choices in your life, based on the appeal of glamour, and had them come back to hurt you?

Do you get image fixes associated with buying and spending?

1. Does there seem to be no end to your desire to buy things?
2. No matter how final your last purchase was, is it only a question of time before you find something else you must have?
3. Do you only feel like a million bucks when you look like you have a million bucks?
4. Do you feel better in the presence of your possessions?
5. Does putting on an expensive piece of jewelry or clothing lift your spirits remarkably?
6. Do you ever think that your problems would be solved if only you could afford that new watch, coat, or car?
7. Do you keep shopping even though you tell yourself that you are going to have to start cutting back?

8. When you're in the process of making a large purchase, do you ever find yourself getting caught up in making an impression on the salesperson?
9. When you are shopping or buying, do you experience a discernible high?
10. How many times have you bought something you couldn't afford and that you really didn't want or need?

Do you get image fixes from the perks associated with your job?

1. Have you lost the ability to make a distinction between a true social life with friends and family and a social life based on business entertaining?
2. Do you enjoy a higher standard of living when you are doing business for the company than you do in your regular life and have you come to count on it?
3. Do the perks of your business make you feel as though you "own the place" even though in reality you have seen other equally "indispensable" people let go with less than a week's notice?
4. Do the perks of your occupation have more appeal than the occupation itself?
5. Does the thought of giving up company perks—car, expense account, etc.—fill you with dread?
6. Do you feel like more of a person because of your expense account?
7. Do the special privileges your company offers—gym privileges, meal privileges, club memberships—make you feel as though you are also "special"?
8. Do you ever feel yourself becoming condescending to-

ward friends whose jobs don't let them eat where you eat, go where you go, drive the car you drive?

9. Does your expense account, in some way, interfere with your relationship with your spouse?
10. Has your need for perks ever caused you to do something you regretted or kept you stuck in a situation for too long?

Are you vulnerable to image fixes associated with status?

1. Do you get as much, or more, pleasure from the prestige associated with your work than you do from the work itself?
2. Do you often find yourself judging people based on their status?
3. When you think about your status or your title, does it give you a special thrill?
4. Is it very important to you to be associated with people you think have status?
5. Do you automatically rule out possible employment opportunities or other options because of the lack of status associated with them?
6. When you tell people what you do for a living, or where you work, do you get a kick out of it when they act impressed?
7. Do you tend to make important purchasing decisions— house, car—based to a large part upon status issues such as neighborhoods or manufacturer?
8. Have you ever spent more money than you could real-

istically afford in order to buy something that carried with it a degree of status?

9. Are you always conscious of where other people went to school and where they work?

10. Have you ever stayed with a job because you were impressed with your title?

11. Have you ever made any important choices (relationships, jobs, surroundings) based on their status appeal and then later had reasons to seriously regret these choices?

If issues of image tend to dominate your thinking, you need to be aware of the possible price you may be paying.

Getting Honest about Whether You Can Afford the Image You Project

"I had this date the other night with a woman who wanted to walk along the beach. I'm wearing a twelve-hundred-dollar suit; I've got a seventy-five-dollar tie; I've got a hundred-and-fifty-dollar shirt; I've got two-hundred-dollar shoes. It costs me fifteen dollars to clean my suit; it costs me six dollars to have my shirt hand washed; I don't want to even think about what it would cost if I should get a drop of spaghetti sauce on my tie. And this woman wants me to roll up my pants and walk along the beach! All I can think about is how much it's going to cost me if she wants to sit down on the sand. Here's the bottom line that I have to ask myself: Can I afford to wear my own clothes?"

—*Stuart, thirty-one, film editor*

Stuart's story is more than an amusing anecdote. It reminds us that, on some level, image always has a price. And it asks a very important question: Can we always afford to pay the price of maintaining these images?

If you are involved with image, it's important to take a careful look at the kind of price you may be paying. Fixes are a crucial part of the system that may be keeping you stuck in an unhappy life-style. For example:

Here are some of the hidden costs that may be associated with power fixes:

- You may find that your need for power is causing you to become detached from yourself and you may suffer a loss of personal authenticity.
- You may lose your ability to relate to others in a genuine and authentic fashion.
- You may lose your perspective on friendships and relationships.
- You may carry your power trip into your home; this can be destructive to your relationships with your family.
- You may find that behavior is required of you that causes you to become a person you wouldn't like very much.
- You may be vulnerable to a loss of power that could leave you seriously shaken and without the necessary emotional skills to cope.
- You may seriously devalue the personal relationships in your life and ultimately find yourself without an emotional support network.
- Your capacity to make logical decisions may be compromised by your need for power.

Here are some of the hidden costs that may be associated with glamour fixes:

• You may be sacrificing real friendships and real relationships.

• You may have a false sense of importance that is likely to evaporate the moment the glamorous surroundings disappear.

• You may find yourself in debt because it's expensive to lead an "exciting" life-style.

• Your attraction to glamour and excitement may make you vulnerable to being exploited by people in power.

• You may find yourself becoming increasingly alienated and detached from your true values.

• You may make important, and fleeting, life choices for all the wrong reasons; these could come back to cause you pain.

Here are some of the hidden costs that may be involved with a pattern of buying and spending:

• You will probably be worried all the time about bills and may feel as though you are never at peace.

• You may suffer from physical or psychological ailments caused by worry.

• Your pattern of spending may leave you with insufficient money with which to make real quality-of-life improvements.

• Your spending habits may be keeping you on an exhausting treadmill.

• You may be expending so much money trying to make money that you have little time left over for creative thinking.

• You may be depriving your family of necessities.

- Poor money management may leave you unable to cope with sudden emergencies.
- You may be trapped in a job because you can't give up the salary.
- You may be losing valuable investment opportunities because of a chronic shortage of money.
- If you have children, you may be giving them a poor set of values.
- You will probably find yourself "stuck" with a host of objects you don't like, can't afford, wish you you could return, etc.

Here are some of the hidden costs of the expense account fix:

- You may fail to adequately account for the fact that some truly terrible jobs have some truly terrific perks.
- You may discover that you are part of a pseudo social world that disappears the moment the expense account disappears.
- You may feel an unwarranted sense of responsibility to your company because of all they "give" you.
- You may be using the perks as a rationalization to avoid the real issues of your employment, such as salary and work load.
- You may feel as though you are living two lives—work life with its perks and home life with realities; this is alienating to your family and loved ones.
- You may have a false sense of importance that disappears the moment you lose the work-associated perks.
- You may discover that too much of your identity is com-

ing from your company-associated perks and consequently lose some of your own sense of self.

• Your thinking and your values may be compromised because you are placing too much value on your perks.

Here are some of the hidden costs when your fixes are derived from status:

• You may find yourself locked into an expensive high-status system that you cannot financially afford.

• You may fail to pursue interesting and valuable job experiences because there isn't enough status associated with them.

• You may create a subtle (or not so subtle) atmosphere of never-ending pressure at home forcing your children and/or spouse to "keep up."

• You may be depriving your life of richness by not opening yourself up to worthwhile people who "don't measure up" or experiences that don't pass the status test.

• You may always find yourself vulnerable to being deflated by someone—often from the same group that made you so status conscious in the first place.

• You may find yourself alienated from real relationships because you can't stop yourself from judging people based on status.

• You may find yourself questioning your own value every time you fail to measure up to your own status needs.

• You may find that you have made important life choices based on status values; these may ultimately boomerang on you.

Getting Honest about the Myths That Drive You

When you believe strongly in a myth and are ultimately disappointed, it is very similar to believing strongly in a person and being disappointed. You put so much energy, time, and faith into the myth that you don't want to let go of it. To admit that the myth is not going to "come through for you," is a little like saying that there is no Santa Claus. And just about everyone wants to believe in Santa Claus. We want to keep the child inside of us alive. On some level, we want to stay vulnerable and open and trusting. We want to believe.

What this means is that, even as the myth is failing us, we set up a very strong bond with it, a form of dependency on it. It becomes almost an addiction, something we don't want to let go of, because to us it represents the part of us that is still capable of a childlike faith.

Getting honest about our myths requires more than an intense examination of the ways in which myths have influenced our thinking. It requires examining the way our myths make us feel and behave. It means acknowledging our disappointment and our sense of failure when our own lives don't play out in accordance with the myths we cherish.

You see, many of the myths we live by are so ingrained into our belief systems that when they fail to work for us, we don't abandon the myth as unworkable. Instead we blame ourselves for our inability to live up to the myth. We behave toward the myth somewhat like obsessed suitors whose love is unrequited. Unable to walk away and let it go, we continue to chase after it, all the while attempting to prove our worthiness. We don't abandon the myth but frequently in the process of pursuing it, we abandon ourselves. Instead of scrutinizing the myth, we scrutinize ourselves. No matter how much evidence is available, we resist finding the myths unrealistic, preferring to find our own attempts to reach it as inadequate.

Were you influenced by the myth of the ''economy with no top end''?

Right now you may be overwhelmed by a sense of downward mobility, or chronically frustrated by economic developments that don't mesh with your belief system. Your distress is the direct result of making basic decisions about what you could spend and what you could afford based on the assumption that the overall economy would continue to grow at a fairly steady rate, and your earning capacity would grow accordingly.

Many of us find it difficult to confront this myth, because we feel almost unpatriotic when we do so. We worry that we are implying that we don't truly believe in the economic future of our country. We have all been raised to believe in the spirit of free enterprise and many of us think that ''getting more tomorrow'' is our inalienable right. To question this makes us feel negative, pessimistic, and full of gloom and doom. Even when the newspapers are saying that everything is on a downward turn, we search out those voices that continue to feed our myth.

For most of us, the issue is not what we should believe about the overall economic picture. What we have to concentrate on is the truth about our own personal economic picture. Whether the economy surges ahead or grinds to a halt, we have to remind ourselves of what we can afford today, not what we will be able to afford tomorrow.

Here are some questions to ask yourself:

- Is your current spending level in sync with your current earning level?
- Are your life-style choices appropriate for someone with your current earning level? Or do you think like someone who earns more than you do and approach the world as if you earn more than you do?
- Are you financially set up to take care of yourself no matter what happens with the general economy?
- Have you placed your economic hopes on a belief that the economy will turn around?
- Do you blame yourself for your economic woes? Do you believe you just didn't move fast enough or get far enough along on your career path before the crunch hit?

Were you influenced by the Horatio Alger myths?

Horatio Alger brings myth into the marketplace, introducing an element of the heroic to anyone who is struggling to get ahead. At the same time, acting as though you are a Horatio Alger hero—working hard, trusting that you will ultimately be rewarded for your excellence and good intentions on some very real level—leaves you open for a great deal of disappointment and frustration. Many of us grew up regarding the Horatio Alger myth as a definite promise: everyone who behaved accordingly would reach his destination. When it doesn't happen we feel overwhelmingly frustrated and disappointed. We don't know whom to blame.

Here are some questions to ask yourself:

• Have you romanticized your career path, turning it into a larger-than-life quest?

• Have you ever done more than your share at work because you thought someone was going to reward you?

• Do you sometimes find yourself bitter and angry because nobody is rewarding your pursuit of the American dream?

• Do you sometimes feel yourself exploited for your good intentions, and then do you get angry at yourself for thinking that way?

• Have you frequently found yourself working for less than you deserve because you thought in the end there would be justice, here on this earth, and it would all be worth it?

• Has your pursuit of career goals isolated you from a here-and-now life?

• If you have failed to reach your goals, do you blame yourself because perhaps you haven't worked hard enough, or done enough to prove yourself?

Have you been unduly influenced by self-help mythology?

When things aren't going according to plan, it seems to make sense to look for some form of advice that will make everything better. Certainly, as writers, we hate to discourage people from buying books. Nonetheless, it seems wise to be wary of very simple answers to very complex problems. To a certain degree, just about everyone is vulnerable to falling into this trap. We all need to be able to admit to ourselves when we do this and recognize the degree to which we can become seduced by this type of information.

Here are some questions to ask yourself:

• Have you ever numbed your pain with self-help bromides that promise more than they can deliver?

• Have you ever substituted wishful thinking for logical thinking?

• Have you ever tried to think, visualize, or wish something into existence and, when it didn't happen, blamed yourself for not thinking, visualizing, or wishing hard enough?

Have you been impressed by a mythology that says "real players and real winners go for it"?

If you have a competitive streak, it's smart to be honest enough to acknowledge the ways in which the concomitant behavior is not always constructive. If you are anxious to get ahead financially, no matter how philanthropic the rationale, it's smart to acknowledge the element of greed that may be attached to your goals. Otherwise your unchecked scenarios for winning might set you up for larger losses down the road. Some of these losses might reflect themselves in your finances; others primarily affect your quality of life.

When you believe it is important to be a "player" and/or a "winner," you should take special pains always to be honest about the trade-offs that you may be making. Are you fully prepared for the consequences of risk taking? Are you truly and honestly prepared for all the consequences of losing? Are you fully prepared for the ways in which thought patterns that revolve around winning and losing will affect your personal life?

Here are some questions to ask yourself:

• Do you dare make a list of what you risk losing in your attempts to win the big prizes you seek?

- Do you put too much value on being viewed as a winner?
- Are you unduly concerned about being viewed as a loser?
- Have you ever had the experience of fearlessly jumping into some venture with the end result of hitting a "bottom" that you never thought would be there?
- When you think about your ability to "go for it" do you feel a sense of pride that overrides common sense?
- Does not being a "player" bring up the same kind of feelings of being excluded when you didn't make the cut in high school?

Have you constructed your very own real estate myths?

There is something very primal about the need to have one's own little piece of turf. Add to that the many messages we have all received about the importance of home ownership and real estate. Everyone has heard stories about the person who established his or her financial security by paying $5,000 to purchase the right house in the right part of town, making it possible to sell the very same property for half a million dollars five years later. These are very compelling messages. Yet we also have abundant information about people who lost their shirts in real estate by buying at the wrong time, buying in the wrong place, or buying at the wrong rate.

What you have to think about is what you really need and what you really want. And do you need what you want? You need to be clear about the emotional issues that may be connected to your real estate agendas. There is a difference between finding a comfortable and attractive place to live and finding a property that has the potential of making (or losing) money. One is shelter; the other is speculation. We need to examine the feelings that are evoked by being a renter or being an owner.

If you personally bought a house that declined in value after the market went down, you need to examine your feelings about this. Here are some questions to ask yourself:

• Some experts now tell us that the most important thing to ask yourself when buying a place to live is whether you'll enjoy living there, not whether you'll be able to make a profit from it. Do you believe this?

• Do you feel that without real estate equity you're nothing?

• Are you unreasonably envious of people who bought real estate when it was still possible to buy real estate?

• Do you experience such waves of real estate envy that you ultimately feel ashamed?

• Do you have an unusual number of real estate fantasies?

• Does the prospect of never owning the house/condo/co-op of your dreams fill you with a sense of complete insecurity?

• Do you have a whole range of unreasonable reactions to your real estate situation such as blaming your family for not owning enough, or feeling guilty because you didn't make the right decisions or didn't have enough money?

• Even though in much of the country the price of real estate has gone down, if that has happened to your house do you feel a sense of personal blame or shame? Do you acknowledge how unrealistic that is?

• Does the possible devaluing of your home terrify you?

• Does your attitude toward real estate leave you vulnerable to episodes of poor judgment when it comes to purchasing and selling?

Are you able to acknowledge your own "yuppie" moments?

Probably if we all had to meet all the criteria attached to being yuppies, there would be an insignificant number of us. Yet there is no question that we have all been affected deeply by the emergence of the yuppie syndrome and all it means. We have to get honest about how much the idealization of so-called yuppie behavior, i.e., the acquisition of more and more, better and better stuff has impacted (to use a yuppie word) on our lives.

Much as we may individually decry the superficiality of the yuppie way of being, few of us are totally free from yuppie urges. We need to be honest about the ways in which we are influenced by the advertising and promotional campaigns that promise us a better "life-style" if we purchase the appropriate product. And we need to be honest about whether or not we can realistically afford to act on these urges.

Here are some questions to ask yourself:

- Do you think of yourself as a yuppie?
- Do you think there are people who would think of you as a yuppie?
- Are you secretly envious of the so-called yuppie life-style?
- Do you feel envious of the so-called yuppie purchasing power?
- Have you indulged in any of the "life-style choices" or purchases that are associated with the yuppies?
- Are you personally impatient about "having it all"?
- Are you anxious about being able to acquire "stuff" while you can "still enjoy it"?

• Do you know many people who would describe themselves as yuppies?

• Do you feel that there is something wrong with you that
you were unable to achieve the so-called yuppie life-style?

Did you construct a mythology around the no-fail professional path?

When your life plan seems to come with so many built-in
guarantees of success, status, and comfort, it comes as a real
shock to the system when it all doesn't pan out as promised.
If your no-fail life plan is failing you, you have to be able to
confront what happened. If you have invested time and effort
into your career, if you did everything you were told to do, it
is understandable why you may now feel betrayed, confused,
and frightened. Working through your feelings is often the first
step in making the necessary adjustments to improve your life,
but it's difficult to deal with all this emotional stuff while you
are still trying to achieve your goals.

First, you need to be able to honestly appreciate how much
you have accomplished, even if you haven't received the rewards you were told to expect. You need to know that you
didn't fail; the world changed. You need honestly to evaluate
your earning potential at this moment. And you need to cope
with those changes you may have to make. Do you want to
change everything, or can you still make it work with modi-
fications? Should you move, retrain, or change a few specifics,
such as leaving private practice and joining a company, or vice
versa? You need to be able to make an honest evaluation of
your choices and their potential, free from feelings of doubt
and self-blame.

Here are some questions to ask yourself:

- Did you choose your career because it came with certain life-style or success guarantees that were either stated or implied?
- If you knew your choice of a profession would not have brought the security you expected, would you still have made the same choice?
- Do you enjoy your work enough to enjoy it even during those times that it may not be bringing you the rewards you feel you were promised?
- Are you able to let go of unfulfilled expectations without feeling that you personally failed in some way?
- Are you emotionally able to make small changes that may improve your situation?

Are you a woman who bought into the myth of "having it all"?

Women don't always admit it, but the truth is that most still have large remnants of this myth hanging around in their psyches. Women were told they could have it all, and they want it all—perfect love, perfect children, perfect career, perfect family life, perfect house, perfect clothes. A great deal in our society continues to reinforce this myth, no matter what. Remember *Baby Boom* with Diane Keaton? She gave up her big fancy career, proving that you can't have it all. But then she kept the baby, started her own successful business, and landed Sam Shepard, thereby proving that you can *really* have it all.

What this means is that if you are a typical woman, you have to acknowledge your most unrealistic fantasies as being just fantasies. Here are some questions to ask yourself:

- Does a stubborn voice inside you still say you can have it all or do it all in spite of all the evidence around you to the contrary?
- Do you fully understand the demands of motherhood?
- Do you fully understand the demands of a career?
- Do you feel like a failure if you are not perfectly juggling it all?
- Do you believe that some women out there are able to do it all, even if you are not?
- Do you look at other women and think that they have been able to accomplish things you have not? How realistic is this?
- Are you able to admit all the ways in which you blame yourself for not being the "perfect woman"?

Getting Honest about Getting Close to the Financial Edge

"We knew we were in serious trouble when we started charging food at Bloomingdale's. After we paid our monthly bills we had so little money left that we used to use charge cards to go to the movies, which, of course, added to the charge card bill."

—*Susan and Mike*

From listening to the conversations around us, it seems as though just about everybody has a rocky financial life. But while knowing that Donald Trump has unmanageable debts may be soothing on some level, it isn't going to help you deal with your bills and your own economic terror.

Susan, a thirty-four-year-old owner of a small boutique and her husband, Mike, a high school music teacher, are typical of many couples who felt confident that two incomes meant they were going to have enough money. For a long time, they tried to avoid reality and failed to evaluate their financial situation honestly. Now they are discovering what it means to be living on the edge. They are very quick to acknowledge that they didn't squarely face their financial situation until it was too late. Susan says:

"We felt as though we talked about nothing but money, but what we were really talking about was our financial anxiety. Our conversations would usually go like this: One of us would start carrying on about how worried he or she was. Then the other one would start being anxious too. Then one of us would start being "supportive" and reassure the other one that everything would be okay if we could just hang on long enough. Then we'd change the subject. We never really sat down and set up a budget and stuck to it."

Nothing increases the likelihood of financial disaster more than a refusal to examine what is going on. Here are some questions to ask yourself:

- Are you in an almost constant state of financial anxiety?
- Do you avoid adding up everything you owe because you don't want to face the truth?
- Are you so worried about conserving cash that you are purposely using your credit cards whenever possible?
- Are you, for example, charging necessities such as food?
- Do you have so many credit lines that you have a hard time remembering exactly how much you owe?

- Are you having a difficult time making your minimum payments?
- Are you without meaningful savings?
- Have you run out of cash credit?
- Is more than 20 percent of your income going for non-mortgage debt?
- Do you owe money—that you can't really repay—to friends or family?
- Do you have any "secret" debts that you're ashamed to talk about, to *anybody?*

All of these indicate that you are not financially prepared for a crisis, and the time has come to deal with it realistically. Even Donald Trump needs help managing his debt, and you may need help with yours.

We, of course, are not financial advisors, but there are certain suggestions that financial planners often make about how and where you should spend your money. For example, many advise monthly payments on your total debt—this means everything added together (mortgage, home equity loans, student loans, auto payments, personal loans)—should not exceed 35 percent of your monthly gross. If you let your debts exceed that limit, you are running a risk. Of this amount, mortgage bankers suggest that no more than 25 to 28 percent of your gross monthly salary should go for your mortgage. Right now financial advisors are telling their clients to reduce their revolving credit card payments to zero because none of the interest is currently deductible. It should be paid off every month. If you can't, the time has come to stop charging.

Getting Honest about Getting Help

Do you need help? Are you honest enough with yourself to admit when you need professional guidance? When your life seems upsetting, depressing, and/or unmanageable, the most important self-admission you can make is the one that has to do with looking for and getting the help you need. This is a tough admission for men and women who consider themselves strong and capable.

Fact: if your situation is scary, complex, and problematic, you need a strong support system to keep emotional balance in your life. It's a mistake to believe that you *have* to do it all alone. You have to be honest enough to acknowledge to yourself that you are not a pillar of stone; you are a human being who needs the emotional help of other human beings who understand your situation. Many people tell us in retrospect that breaking through their own resistance and admitting to themselves that they needed help was the hardest step in the process of putting balance back into their lives. Yet it's also the necessary first step. The second one is finding the help you need.

Complicated situations require complicated solutions. And this may mean reaching out to various types of help, whether simultaneously or sequentially. One invaluable source of assistance can be found in the professional helping networks. When possible, it's best to start looking for a therapist through the process of referral. Churches, hospitals, and the department of social services can also furnish you with a number of good referrals.

It is sometimes possible to find a therapist or counselor who offers his or her services on a sliding-scale fee. This type of assistance is most easily found in conjunction with universities or other teaching facilities where counselors are in *supervised* internships.

For those of you who are married or involved in an important long-term relationship, some type of couples counseling may be extremely helpful, if not vital. If you fear revealing your struggle to your partner, couples therapy provides the safest forum for that kind of honesty. If there are conflicts in the way you and your partner perceive your professional positions, your spending habits, your attitudes toward money, status, or image, couples counseling is again probably the safest place to begin examining these differences.

For example, if one of you is a spender and the other a saver, you have a problem as a couple. If one of you is running up the credit card bills and the other is bailing you out, you have a couples' problem. If one of you expects the other to be entirely responsible for all financial aspects of your relationship, you have a couples' problem. If you disagree about the best way to manage your finances, you have a couples' problem. If one of you wants to sell the house, and the other can't give it up, you have a couples' problem. If one of you has created financial anxiety in any way from running up debt to avoiding taxes, you have a problem as a couple. And couples' issues are best addressed as a couple.

Of course, you could try to work these things out as a couple without the use of any professional or nonprofessional support. This type of work is extremely tricky and even the best attempts at negotiating a couple's issues can break down very quickly if feelings are hurt or ignored, if fantasies are shattered, if the discussion becomes accusatory, etc. For this reason, we strongly encourage you to seek some type of third-party intervention and support for addressing these issues. If your struggle is affecting other family members as well and you do not know how to approach these family members, there are many people who specialize in family systems who can be of tremendous assistance to you.

Couples counselors are best found through a referral from someone you trust and respect, but there are various other means as well (through your church or synagogue, through your physician, through a local university, through the department of social services, etc.). Remember that there is nothing wrong with "shopping around." No one therapist works for everyone; what you are looking for is a good "fit"—a therapeutic relationship that feels comfortable and trusting for both of you.

Professional help is extraordinarily beneficial if you can obtain it, but it is far from the only resource. We feel very strongly that no individual who is struggling with an unmanageable life should discount the benefits to be gained from the nonprofessional network of available help. This includes the various twelve-step programs (based on the twelve steps of recovery formulated by the extraordinarily successful Alcoholics Anonymous program). Organized and run by members, these all revolve around the premise of anonymity. Some programs worth considering are:

Codependents Anonymous (CODA): For men and women who find themselves involved in addictive, needy, unfulfilling, or destructive relationship patterns relating back to dysfunctional family backgrounds.

Shopaholics Anonymous: For men and women who are unable to control their spending.

Alcoholics Anonymous: For men and women with substance-abuse problems.

Narcotics Anonymous: For men and women with substance-abuse problems.

Adult Children of Alcoholics (ACA, ACOA): For men and women suffering from the effects of growing up in an alcoholic or otherwise dysfunctional household.

Overeaters Anonymous (OA): For men and women who get their "fix" from food.

Gamblers Anonymous: For men and women who can't control their gambling.

Al-Anon: For friends and family of alcoholics.

These programs address a much broader audience than one might imagine. Take CODA for example. One has a tendency to think of codependency as being limited to people who are in addictive love relationships. What few people recognize until they get to a CODA meeting is that codependency issues can emerge in a wide variety of situations —with coworkers, employers, employees, family, and friends.

And you don't have to be losing your shirt in Las Vegas to benefit from Gamblers Anonymous. Many people handle money in such a way that they are always on the edge. They may overbuy, overinvest, overborrow. All of these issues are addressed in these meetings. Facing your subtle (or not so subtle) addictions or dependencies could prove to be a vital part of your "uncrippling."

Twelve-step programs are being run in thousands of cities and towns throughout the United States. Meeting times and information can be obtained through your local church or synagogue, through hospitals, or by contacting the closest office of Alcoholics Anonymous. Meetings can be found at a variety of locations, almost any day of the week, often at various times during the day and night. Meetings are member supported, but support is purely voluntary (members typically contribute somewhere between fifty cents and one dollar per meeting).

8

Success Means . . .

◰

"The good life is a process, not a state of being. It is a direction, not a destination."

—*Carl Rogers*

Some people might argue that if you are a functioning human being on this planet, you have already achieved some measure of success, and let it go at that. Most of us are not all that easy on ourselves, and few of us ever reach the point where we are able to perceive ourselves as being successful. No matter how much you have accomplished, it is unlikely that you think of yourself as a success. For example, if you were to query a group of multimillionaires, a fairly large percentage of them would still see success as something in their future, not their present. They are still looking for more—more money, more achievement, more status, more personal satisfaction, more recognition, or more creative fulfillment.

One of the most complicated things about success is that we are not really sure exactly what constitutes a successful life. Should we look at a person's accomplishments, or should we concentrate on how satisfied or happy he or she feels? How can we tangibly measure success? The fact is that we have very few good role models for how to lead a successful life, and we're not sure precisely where to look for guidance.

It would appear that the vast majority of us should take a fresh look at what it means to be successful. We need to reorient our thinking so that we can realistically feel we are leading successful lives *right now,* without having to earn any more money, buy any more stuff, or reach any new heights. In short, if we want to lead more fulfilled lives, we need to decide for ourselves what it is that makes us feel good about who we are *right now* and what we are doing *right now.* Each of us needs to write new definitions of success that work for his or her life.

It may seem simple or even trite, but the truth is that redefining success means looking at your life and appreciating all the ways in which you are already a success. In other words, it means establishing parameters for success on your own terms—writing your own definition of success by deciding for yourself what works for you.

SCENARIOS FOR SUCCESS:
FINDING A NEW DEFINITION

Success Means . . . Accepting
Yourself for Who You Are

Self-acceptance is the first step on the road to a successful life. It's time to start celebrating who you are, appreciating who you are, and liking who you are. Self-acceptance means that you can no longer focus on the person you think you should be, the person your parents think you should be, the person who society thinks you should be, or the person you plan to be someday in the near or distant future. Enjoy who you are right now, not who you will be when you make that big deal, get that partnership, or buy that house.

Psychology has struggled for years with the conflict between the ideal self and the real self. In fact, for many it is the stuff of therapy, the stuff that can cause the most profound distress. You can spend your entire life anticipating who you eventually want to be, but in the process you may fail to appreciate all that is special and wonderful in your life at this very moment.

Some men and women are terrified of this notion, because to them it means giving up the quest, giving up the dream. It's important to remember that acceptance isn't about giving up. It's about finding the joy in your life by coming to terms with where you live right now, what you do for a living right now, how much money you have right now, what you do or don't own, right now. Without that sense of self-acceptance, no one can ever feel successful.

Success Means . . . Being Able to Be Honest with Yourself and with Those around You

It's a given: As long as you shroud all your problems in secrecy and shame and are unable to face yourself squarely and honestly, a sense of success will evade you.

The value of this kind of honesty is something that has been pointed out to us time and again by the many twelve-step programs that have been undeniably effective for millions of men and women. If you get involved with one of these programs, one of the crucial first steps that you are expected to take is the admission that your life is out of control. This admission is essential to one's recovery within the program and is an integral part of all of these ''anonymous'' groups.

In these programs, acknowledging shortcomings and self-doubt to yourself is not enough; you must tell others as well. And there are very good reasons for this. The creators of these programs understood that as long as we were able to deceive those around us, we were likely, at least on some level, to continue to deceive ourselves as well. Once our problems are out in the open, the burden is lifted. The need for deception is no longer there, and the likelihood of self-deception is greatly reduced. As long as one is denying one's truths, there can never be a true sense of self, let alone a sense of success.

None of us is so perfect that we couldn't tolerate a reasonable amount of self-scrutiny. It's a rare person who isn't hiding something. Many of us fail to realize the burden of self-deception or the kind of price we may be paying. Self-examination—whether it's done in a support group, a therapist's office, a place of worship, or the privacy of your own living room—is often the secret key that will allow you to open the doors to a sense of self-fulfillment and personal satisfaction.

Success Means . . . That You Will No Longer Put Off Living

This is the big trap we all fall into. Virtually everyone who has any interest in this book knows, on some level, that he or she has been putting off life. Sacrificing, avoiding, displacing—all the things we do because we are too busy to do anything else.

What do we put off? We put off relationships, love, friendships, and personal growth. We put off developing interests, furthering talents, and fostering creativity. We put off days in the country and we put off getting enough sleep. We keep anticipating tomorrow and forgetting about right now. But if you're not living in the here-and-now, you're not living. This may not be perfect, but it is yours to savor at this moment.

Being able to live in the present is the real proof of success, and it's something you can start doing immediately. The phrase "being in the moment" has been used to death, but there is a reason why so many people keep coming back to it—it's the essence of having a real life. So we're throwing it at you again and hoping that this time it will stick.

Success Means . . . Knowing All the Ways in Which You Are Already a Winner

Five years ago, Scott was a hungry young man, hungry for traditional success, hungry for money, hungry for the company of glamorous women, hungry for more. At the age of thirty, he had his own law practice, a comfortable condo, a nifty sports car, a house at the shore, and a boat. Tall, handsome, articulate, and charming, he seemed to be the quintessential eligible bachelor, straight out of central casting. He behaved accordingly, surrounding himself with more women than even he could keep track of and rarely dating anyone more than two or three times.

Although Scott had a very active social life, and a very lucrative career, many people who knew him complained that he was arrogant. They found his emphasis on "winning and losing" intimidating and grating. In fact, few of his contemporaries felt they could "keep up with him." But Scott didn't care; he was a "winner" and that's all that mattered to him.

Now, at thirty-five, Scott is a totally different human being. You see, when Scott was thirty-one, he was stricken with a particularly virulent form of leukemia. Everything in his life changed. And he changed accordingly. To his credit, he was able to make the leap, evaluate his priorities, and reorganize his life without bitterness or irrational anger. He says:

"In many ways, getting sick was a very good thing for me. It forced me to realize what was really important. In terms of illness and treatment, I've had it all. I've been in remission twice, and I've had the disease come back twice. I've had chemotherapy, radiation therapy, bone marrow therapy. I've been in the hospital for months on end. I've made good friends there. I've seen people die, but I've also seen people live, and I've learned a great deal. I've learned what's important and what's not."

In the course of his illness, Scott realized the importance of commitment and love, and he married one of the women he was dating. Four months ago, his wife gave birth to an extraordinarily beautiful child. Together they are living and dealing with their struggle one day at a time. Scott says he has learned to enjoy everything he can:

"Right now, I'm in remission. Maybe it will last a lifetime, maybe it won't. Because of the last therapy I received, which is fairly experimental, but very successful when it works, I'm told I have a very good shot at a normal life span. But whatever happens, I'm never again going to do what I did. For example, I'm taking six months off right now to be with my wife and child. We're fortunate. We didn't get into any big overhead. We don't have a big house, or big cars, or any big expenses, and I'm going to keep it that way. I'm always going to keep it so that we can spend time together.

"When the question becomes one of life and death, you realize that you don't really need that much to live on. You realize what it really means to be a winner. Now, I take simple little walks, and I savor them. I know how close I came to losing that. I want to enjoy every moment of every day. I don't want to drive myself. I want to spend time with my wonderful wife and my wonderful baby, and I don't need the rat race."

In the course of writing this book, we spoke to a fair number of people who suffered near-fatal illnesses. To a person, they voiced exactly the same sentiments, saying that the experience of almost losing their lives helped them helped them reshape and rebalance themselves. One of them, a forty-six-year-old woman, said:

"Sometimes I say that cancer was the best thing that ever happened to me because once you have cancer or any illness which is genuinely life threatening, it puts everything else in perspective. I wouldn't wish the cancer part on anyone, but in many ways it ultimately improved my life because I really had to think about what was important. Both my husband and I had to change the way we lived. Everything changed, including the way we spend money, relate to each other, relate to the children and the world. I know that I don't have time to worry about petty stuff or whether we're keeping up with the Joneses. I'm happy to be alive. And I'm grateful."

Not everybody has to brush this close to death to realize how much life he or she has, but stories like these can help you understand just how much of a winner you are at this very moment.

Success Means . . . Knowing When to Stop Banging Your Head against the Same Old Brick Wall

"For ten years I tried to get established in the restaurant business. This may not seem like a big deal to some people, but to me, it was everything. My restaurant was my life. And no matter what I did, I couldn't make it do any more than break even. I changed menus, changed staff, reorganized the kitchen. I advertised in print, on the radio. Everything. I was determined. But it didn't work. Finally I threw in the towel. Although I didn't know it at the time, it was the best day of my life."

—Theo, forty-one

For Theo, losing his dream was a liberating experience. It made him acknowledge that his dream had taken over his life. It had become this enormous brick wall against which he threw himself at regular intervals, only to get bruised again and again. Finally he walked away, and when he did, his life changed.

Now Theo is working a regular job, but as he says:

"I'm also working regular hours. I'm saving money. I'm not spending everything I make, telling myself that it doesn't matter because as soon as the business picks up, I'll be able to pay for everything. I've had to get realistic. In the process I've realized that I was killing myself.

"The first few months without the restaurant, I was still numb with the damage I did to myself. My body was so tired that I actually felt bruised. I didn't know how to sleep, how to rest, how to eat. Everything is so much better now, and I'm so glad that I finally had the brains to walk away from it. It was tough; it meant acknowledging defeat. But so what? I'm still the same person."

On some level, walking away from a losing proposition goes against the grain of what we were taught. Everyone remembers the adage, "A winner never quits, and a quitter never wins." Voices in one's head repeat the theme, "If at first you don't succeed, try, try again." All of this is great, if (a) one is dealing with an achievable goal, and (b) the goal is worth the price.

To decide whether a goal is achievable is no small matter. You have to consider a variety of factors that may have nothing to do with your ability or talent. A million and one outside factors, from the economy to the weather, can affect the success or failure of a business or a career.

To decide whether or not your goal is worth the price you are paying is probably a little bit easier. If your goal is destroying your life, then it may be time to walk away and forget about all the outdated messages playing in your head.

Success Means . . . Knowing How to Make the Small Improvements That Can Alter the Quality of Your Life

"On bad days, I want to change everything, from the color of my hair to what I do for a living. I want a whole new life, a whole new wardrobe. And I want it in a whole new city. Unrealistic, huh?"

—*Stephanie, thirty-nine*

Everyone can change his or her life. The question is how much and how fast. Many of us are like Stephanie; we envision change as something sweeping to the point of exhilaration. We want immediate results. We want to be able to make the decision for change, and then experience an incredible upheaval that brushes away everything that is unpleasurable and leaves us embracing a glorious new existence. But the truth is that change rarely happens in this fashion, and it is often suspicious when it does.

When we are unhappy in our lives, we frequently are able to think only in absolutes. We don't know how to make tomorrow a little bit better because we want everything to be monumentally better. So instead of thinking about what we can do in the next hour that will make that hour better, we fantasize about large changes that we don't have the ability to immediately implement. By viewing change only in giant steps, we paralyze ourselves and block ourselves from taking all those little steps that are the stuff that real change is made of.

Karen, the owner of a small costume-jewelry store, is a

good example of someone who has been able to change her life without changing everything. During the recent recession, her business dwindled, drastically cutting her income. At first she didn't know what to do. She planned to close the store and go out of business, but that was frightening, and seemed to be too drastic a step. There was always the possibility that business would improve, and she didn't want to throw it all away. So she devised a plan for the store that was essentially a holding action. She had always had two employees. So what she did immediately was to let one of them go. The other she kept on, with the stipulation that the woman would basically run the store on her own. Business was consistently dropping off, so her work load was not overwhelming even though she was alone.

For herself, Karen had another plan. She applied to a graduate program in public health—something that she is able to do evenings and weekends. One day a week, Karen works in an antique store near where she lives, earning a little extra money. And she has taken a temporary roommate, thereby cutting her living expenses. All of these changes have placed Karen in the position where she has several options open to her, depending upon what happens with the economy.

For most of us, there are usually a variety of things we can do that will add on possibilities, rather than take them away. For example, you may not need to change your job to feel better. Perhaps you only need to work fewer hours each week and use the extra hours to evaluate your future. Perhaps you don't need to sell your house and move. Maybe you can economize in a combination of other ways that, added together, will have the same effect. In order to make constructive life changes, you have to get honest about those small things that can make a major difference. You have to figure out what they are and then honestly try to implement them even if you can only do that the smallest bit at a time.

We need to realize that sometimes there are only very fine lines marking the difference between comfort and discomfort. Crossing those lines may not be as difficult as we think. We've all had the experience, for example, of sitting in a chair or a couch and feeling uncomfortable. Something isn't quite right. And then somebody miraculously comes along and changes one thing. Perhaps it's the lighting. Maybe it's an extra pillow. Perhaps it was too hot or cold in the room, and the thermostat needed adjusting. Whatever that change was, it was like a miracle. Suddenly you felt better; in fact, you felt terrific.

For most of us, changing little things about our lives can have the same kind of powerful results. So you have to stop thinking only in terms of grandiose, absolute, large-scale, momentous, earth-shattering change, and you have to start getting honest about those specific, concrete, small things that can make your day-to-day real life better.

Remember those small changes can change your attitude and make it possible for you to make those big changes you dream about. And, even more important, small changes in and of themselves often add up in a way so that their cumulative effect is much greater than the sum of their parts.

Success Means . . . Finding the Time and Energy to Develop Your Own Creativity

Creativity is a misunderstood concept. All too often, a person decides that unless one can write like Hemingway, sing like

Streisand, paint like Van Gogh, or dance like Baryshnikov, he or she should give up on the creative process and leave it to the geniuses, or at least very talented experts. In truth, we are all creative. Remember the joy you felt when you were a child and you were able to indulge your need to draw, paint, sculpt, make music, or dance? Remember how much fun it was to bang away on your cymbals, or mix differing amounts of blue and yellow to produce the precise shade of green you wanted to paint your very own tree?

To one degree or another, every single one of us is creative, and in order to lead successful lives, we need to act on these creative impulses. Some people are able to find their creativity in activities that are also useful; designing and sewing a new outfit is a good example. Gardening is another way to be creative and practical. So are activities such as woodworking and home repair. But a fair number of people need creative outlets that serve no visibly useful purpose—making art that no one will ever buy, shaping pottery that no one will ever use, or writing songs that no one will ever record. This is fun. This allows each one of us, for a moment or two, to feel like Picasso or at least like the children we once were.

And for some fortunate people, developing creativity can sometimes spell out the route to finding a new way to earn a living. Tracy, forty-three, is one such person. She says:

"I think on some level I've always been a frustrated artist, but I didn't know it. For years I earned my living selling advertising space. Nothing creative about that job. But I thought I wanted to write, so I would work on novels, plays, poetry—none of which ever earned me any money. Then about four years ago, I started taking classes in painting—one evening a week after work. I really enjoyed it, so I got more

adventurous and took a more advanced class on Saturday—
one that was closer to professional level. My teacher encouraged me a great deal, and I spent more and more of my free
time painting. Six months ago, I was in my first real art show.
And just last week, I got a gallery to handle my work. I'm
starting to sell now, and I believe I can see a time when I will
be able to earn my living this way. But even if I couldn't earn
a penny, I'm not about to stop painting. I love it too much.''

What Tracy realized as she became more involved with art
is that the creative process is a form of meditation that can put
you in touch with your own inner core. So whether you're
planting snapdragons, constructing a bookcase, building your
own computer, or singing off key, it's important to stay in
touch with the part of you that is uniquely creative.

Success Means . . . Not Feeling As Though You Have to Apologize for What You Do, What You Make, or What You're Called

''For years a part of me was always ashamed of where I was
in terms of my career. I had friends who made more than I
did, friends who had more important jobs than I did and
friends who I thought were leading more productive lives
than I was. I remember when I felt as though I was apolo-
gizing because I didn't own my own co-op; then when I
finally got a co-op, I felt as though I should apologize
because it wasn't grand enough. Then last year, I had lunch
with two of these friends, and we started talking—really
talking. I discovered that they felt the same way. That's

why one of them is now struggling with this major mortgage, trying to pay for an oversized house. The other one is
a VP in a big company—he said he was ashamed that he
never made senior VP. That's when I decided that this
business of always feeling as if I had to do more, do better,
was ruining my life. It was robbing me of so much pleasure.
I vowed I was going to change my attitude. And I have.
Like Popeye said, 'I am what I am, and that's all that I am.'
That should be enough.''

—Hank, forty-four, advertising writer

A primary reason why we want to be successful is so we can
feel successful. That means that when someone asks what we
do, we will feel a surge of pride, not twinges of insecurity and
ambivalence. Why do we get embarrassed about where we are
in relation to the rest of the world? This is another place where
image comes in. We see the glamorous men and women on the
TV; we pick up magazines and newspapers and we read about
people who seem to have it made, men and women with
important titles and large salaries; we see people we know
living in better surroundings, wearing more expensive clothing, taking fancier vacations, and sending their children to
better schools.

As competitive as you may be, you are probably surrounded
by peers who seem even more competitive. So often they share
only the good news about their careers, their purchases, and
their love lives. They don't 'fess up and tell all about the deals
going sour, the problems on the job, or the late payments on
the car. They are so worried about the images they are projecting that they rarely present a true picture of what is going
on in their lives. No wonder so many of us feel so insecure.

Getting rid of this kind of insecurity is a necessary prerequisite to feeling like a success. Insecurities will always make someone vulnerable to manipulation by issues of image. If you are prone to this kind of insecurity, you will never feel like a success, no matter what is achieved or how much money is made.

Success Means . . . Taking Time to Relate to the People You Love

The people you love are the people to whom you should be most responsive and caring. Yet, spouse, lover, parents, children, friends—these are the people who are apt to suffer when you are embarked on a fast career track. When you're busy networking, it's so easy to decide that your nearest and dearest can wait until your career gets up to speed. But can they?

Snapping at one's mate, neglecting one's children, snarling at one's parents, avoiding one's friends—these are the behavior patterns that reflect unhappiness, sometimes because one has not achieved the level of success one wants. Yet, we all realize that we don't need financial security or public acclaim in order to behave in a human way to those around us. The fact is that we can give the people we love and care about the love and care they deserve no matter how well or badly our careers are going. If we can't do that, then we are lost.

Success Means . . . Knowing When to Compete and When to Let Go

"I've had to learn to let go of a lot. A few years back I would fight over every point. I couldn't stop. If I disagreed

with a coworker, I would hammer away. If I had problems with my boss, I would think about it and devise little ways to make my point. It was silly and it was stupid. All I got for my trouble was an ulcer that forced me to change.''
      —Derek, thirty-three, sales representative

Derek's ulcer forced him to become less competitive. Hopefully most of us can learn this lesson in an easier fashion, but this is such a hard lesson to learn. We've all been taught to compete, to do everything we can to win. But there are so many times when the game isn't worth the candle. We all need to learn to save our energy for the important battles, and to let go of those things that don't count in the long run. There is so much that happens in the course of our lives that is not ultimately important to our welfare.

Success Means . . . Being Able to Lose Your Career without Losing Yourself

Dale, a forty-two-year-old manager, is someone who has had to totally revise his life plan. He learned that corporate life isn't always secure. He lost his first corporate job during the 1982 recession. Even though he quickly found another, he says that experience taught him it could happen again. And it did.

"By the time I was fired, or laid off, or resigned—whatever you want to call it—I had few illusions that corporate life was going to be a secure situation. Even so, you never really think you're going to be the one who's laid off, particularly if you've always been told—as I was—that you're very good at what you do. But I came to realize that there are policy decisions that have nothing to do with who is best and who is not.''

Before his job ended, Dale had what could be described as a very exciting career. Very involved in the international division of his company, he flew all over the world working on ''glamorous things like joint ventures, divestitures of assets, restructuring of companies''—all the things he loved to get into. He says:

''I had some of the best jobs you could ever have in corporate America. I have no resentment about not getting the nifty jobs because I got all of them.''

Dale and his family were also located in a beautiful community where they made ample use of all the recreational facilities. But that had to change a year ago when Dale lost his job. Unlike many people, Dale was fortunate because he and his wife had some savings, and she was able to get a job.

''My wife is the calmest person about all of this. She never trusted corporations so she wasn't shocked at what happened. She keeps telling me to take my time and find something I want.''

Like many others, Dale and his wife have heavy mortgage debt. Unlike many others, they have been prepared to cut and make drastic changes in their lives.

''We made an apartment over the garage, and rented that out. Then we also rented out an extra room in the house. It's not ideal, and we'd like to have the space, but we do what's necessary. Now we have to be a lot quieter in the mornings. Eventually that may produce a certain amount of strife, but right now it's just a minor inconvenience. Between the two rents, the mortgage payments are pretty much covered.''

For babysitting, Dale and his wife drew up a complicated schedule that includes both of them pitching in. On weeks that Dale schedules many job interviews and meetings, his wife's mother, who lives a couple of hours away, spends the week with them, taking care of the children.

At the end of fifteen months, Dale found that he was still without a job, so he made a choice.

"I figured I could only pretend so long that something was going to happen next week. It didn't. So we took an equity loan on the house and my wife took a loan at work, and we made a bid on a convenience store in a neighboring town. It was accepted.

"This is going to be a whole new life. I think I'm going to like it. It's going to be a lot different from going to work in a suit and tie. But so what? If anything, I'm excited. It's my show, and I see it as a real challenge. Who knows where it will go from here, but I'll worry about that as things evolve."

Dale views his job loss as a chance to embark on a new life plan, and he's looking forward to it. It's apparent from his story that his sense of self was not jeopardized by his job loss, and that his identity was not piggybacking on his professional status. He has turned something that might seem terrifying into something exciting. He will have a strong sense of self no matter what happens with his career.

Success Means . . . Taking Good Care of Yourself

Getting enough sleep, eating properly, exercising regularly— this is basic stuff. But it is the stuff we tend to ignore. There is only one problem: we can't without paying a large price.

Do you need to change your eating habits? Make a sensible plan and start working on it today. Do you need to change your sleeping habits? New research tells us that if you are not waking naturally each morning, you are sleep deprived. Go to bed earlier. Stop making yourself function on too little rest. It will not work in the long run. It's probably not even working now.

Do you need to change your sheets? What kind of environment are you maintaining for yourself? Does your external environment reflect your internal chaos? Do you have a soothing place to come home to or is your home a reminder of everything that isn't going well? It's harder to feel good about yourself if you don't feel good about your surroundings. If necessary, hire a service to get you started, and then stay on top of your personal cleaning and laundry.

Do you need to visit your dentist? Make an appointment. Do you need to see a doctor? Make another appointment.

Just remember what grandma would have said: Take care of your body or your body will take care of you.

Success Means . . . Spending Time with the People Who Care about You

Everyone needs to feel accepted. Acceptance provides a relaxed feeling, a sense of belonging, of contentment and well-being. But where is it that we can go to find acceptance? Where can you come forward secure with the knowledge that you can be your real self? Who are the people to whom you can admit your greatest fears, shortcomings, failures, and anxieties?

The people who come to mind are the ones to whom you don't have to present a polished image, the ones who are happy for your success but who don't view it as a prerequisite to friendship. These are your friends, the people who don't expect you to be superhuman.

If you have only a handful of friends like this in your life, you are extremely fortunate. Yet it is often these very people who are the first we sacrifice when we get caught up in networking and careerism. Instead, we start spending time with people who provide or reflect an image we desire. Now this may start off as a glamorous, enjoyable experience. But unless the relationships deepen, such experiences rarely give us the kind of comfort that we require on an ongoing basis.

Even more disturbing, neglecting our old tried-and-true friendships can make us lose our capacity to be connected to our roots, our own sense of self, and those people who can continue to enrich our lives.

Success Means . . . Controlling Your Finances

Do you assume that once you "hit the top," that's when all the bills will be paid? Big mistake. You don't need to make a lot of money to be in control of your finances. And even more important, unless you are in control of your money, you will never feel as though you are in control of your life.

Often, getting in control of your finances means getting in control of your attitude about your financial image. People frequently are so concerned about how things look that they don't take the necessary steps to save themselves until the problems multiply. Remember that there are always things you can do. If you're having trouble paying the rent or making the mortgage, for example, get a roommate or rent out rooms. In terms of ways of getting extra income, make use of whatever resources you have available. Don't worry about what people will think. Do what you have to do, before things get any worse.

Sometimes getting in control of one's finances means getting outside help. Financial planners and accountants can often help you do just that. Whenever possible, get a second opinion on any financial advice you are given to make certain that it is, indeed, correct and appropriate to your situation. If you have mortgages or outstanding loans, deal with your bank before it gets too late. Frequently they may agree to reduced payments or make some kind of concessions to help you keep your account in order. Banks don't want to foreclose or push people into bankruptcy unless they have no choice. Get in there and negotiate with them and give them a choice.

We realize that it's unrealistic to think that one can iron out one's personal financial mess all that simply. Getting rid of debts takes a great deal of self-control and discipline. You have to make a budget and stay on it. You have to accept the necessity of eating inexpensively. You have to deprive yourself of new clothes and vacations. You have to stop using credit to pay for things you can't afford. You have to watch your pennies as well as your dollars. You have to learn about cash and forego plastic. You may have to relinquish a large number of creature comforts. Sometimes you may be forced to take work that you feel is beneath you, or you may find it necessary to get a part-time second job. But if you do all this, eventually you will pay off your debts, and you will be in control of your finances. Once you begin to see that this is possible, you will feel 100 percent better about everything in your life.

Success Means . . . Finding Time for Real Recreation

Recreation means play time, and nobody can achieve a balanced life without finding time for play. There is a difference between recreation and going out a lot. Some people go out a lot, but it's not really social, it's not really enjoyable, or they're not genuinely involved with the experience. Real recreation means more than just an occasional movie or putting in an appearance at a party. Getting involved with some real recreation means spending time doing those things you enjoy with those people you like in a way that is meaningful to you and to them. That means that you are fully "there" and involved with the experience.

Success Means . . . Knowing That Everything Has Its Price—and Knowing How Much You Are Prepared to Pay

Whether you can put it in dollars and cents or in years off your life, whether you pay for it up front, pay for it in a therapist's office, or pay for it in your old age, everything you are doing now and every choice you are making has a cost. Maintaining an image has a price. So does neglecting your health. Short-change your family and it costs. Neglect your finances and you'll suffer. It's that simple.

So many of us think that we are exempt from the rules. We don't believe that we will ever have to "pay the piper" or we harbor the illusion that we will have ultimate control over what the price will be or when we will be expected to pay it.

It's all a little like interest on a credit card. If you don't pay when you make the purchase and instead choose to make monthly payments, it could all end up costing twice as much. Keep that in mind when you fail to be responsive to your loved ones, or when you neglect your health, or when you lose sight of your true priorities.

Success Means . . .
Letting Go of Envy

Look at those expensive clothes, look at that ring, look at that watch, look at that car, look at that garden, look at that house, look at that life-style, look at what that other person has on his or her plate! Envy is nothing new. It's a perfectly human emotion, although the fact is that envy is one of those emotions that we all wish we didn't have.

Envy is a tough emotion to control, but if you don't control it, it will start controlling you. Envy makes us prisoners of other people's image issues as well as our own. Envy is negative; it keeps you stuck; it keeps you from appreciating the positive aspects of your own life; and it totally distorts your sense of reality.

Success Means . . . Taking Care of Your Own Spiritual Development

"I'm not saying that I found enlightenment or that I totally gave my life and will over to some mysterious kind of power. I couldn't do that. Besides, I feel as though I've been giving my life over to powers outside me all my life. For me, being spiritual was a very personal thing. It meant stopping the external search for validation and hope and starting to look inside of myself. The more I connected with my own insides, the more I felt genuinely spiritual, grounded in a way I wasn't used to experiencing. It was about gaining strength, not giving up. I was able to lose much of my manipulative behavior and get a true sense of my own own strength and my inside. I had to find the part of God that was inside me, not the God that everyone told me was out there."

—Kevin, thirty-four, writer

Some people have a very traditional view of God. Others, like the naturalist, John Muir, feel that they see and are aware of God's presence whenever they are exposed to a tree, a mountain, or any other manifestation of nature. Many people are like Kevin; they don't have a traditional concept of God, but even so they maintain a strong sense of their own place within the ordered disorder of the universe. Whatever you believe, or don't believe, each of us has within us a spirit that needs time and tending. Whether you define it as your connection to the divine, your connection to the planet, or your connection to yourself, taking care of your inner spirit is an essential ingredient to leading a successful life.

Success Means . . . Following a Life Plan That Is Based on Your True Values

It's one thing to decide what's really important to you, it's another thing to act on it. Acting on your true values probably means that you will have to make some changes in the way you behave, and real change means that you need a real plan. It's a little like moving to a new town. When you move to a new place, there are certain things you have to do. You have to establish residency. You have to find new places to shop. You have to make new friends, even if you're terrified. You do it because you have to. It's hard, it takes time, and you often mourn the loss of the old ways. You may even entertain thoughts about returning back to where you were before. But you can't, so you press on.

When you start to realign your life in terms of what is important to you, you have to be very clear about your priorities, and you need a schedule to help you behave accordingly. Sit down with a date book and force yourself to make a schedule of how your ideal week would look—a week that puts proper emphasis on self-development, family development, relationship development, spiritual development.

When you're making your schedule, think also about your emotions and feelings. Think about feelings that you experience too often—feelings such as anxiety, dread, tension, pressure. Make a list of negative feelings and then write down those situations or experiences that regularly provoke those feelings. These are the feelings that, as much as possible, you want to avoid.

Think about those feelings that you don't have enough of in

your life, feelings such as contentment, peace, happiness. Think about laughing. How often do you get to laugh? How often do you need to laugh? Write down a list of good feelings, and then next to each feeling, write down two or three life situations in which you might experience those feelings. These are the feelings that you want more of in your life.

Finally, make a list of the people and ideas that are important to you. Then go about finding ways in your schedule so that the people you care about and the ideas that matter receive their fair share of time and energy.

At the end of each week evaluate your performance. How close did you come to following your ideal schedule? What might make some of the changes easier to enact? Did you spend at least one evening with people you care about interacting in a meaningful way? Did you take an hour to read the book you wanted to read? Did you meditate before you went to sleep? Did you make time for a self-help group that has meaning to you? Did you find time to foster some creative effort? Did the things you were involved with and the people you spent time with reflect your true values?

We need to say right here that if you decide to change your life, simply making that decision isn't going to produce miracles. If there is a difference at all, it will be a glimmer of hope that was not there before. Realistic change is something that happens in stages. You will not wake up next week and feel totally different. But one day, you will wake up and you will be different. Not because something magical happened the night before, not because you had some mystical experience or profound revelation, and not because great fortune suddenly landed at your doorstep. But because you opened yourself up to the slow process of real change.

Success Means . . . Putting
Balance in Your Life

So many people complain that they have no balance in their lives; they say they do nothing but work and worry. If that is how you are feeling right now, you may have to force yourself to create a world for yourself outside of work. Again, this won't be easy. It might be helpful to approach this the same way you'd approach looking for a new job.

When you're looking for a new job, you make a résumé, make inquiries, make appointments, and then follow up. Creating a life beyond work requires many of the same skills and puts you through many of the same experiences. Just as with job hunting, remember that if you put in the hours and time, the odds are that you will reach your goal—you will have a more balanced life.

Right now, if you don't feel that your life is balanced, you are stuck. So what you have to do is get yourself unstuck. You have to start doing things differently. You need to believe that any type of change, no matter how seemingly insignificant, is positive. The only place you can no longer afford to be is exactly where you are. To get your life back into balance, you have to introduce change to disrupt the stagnant equilibrium of your system. You have to force yourself to live in a balanced way. You may have to force yourself, for example, to eat in a balanced way. You may have to force yourself to find appropriate recreational outlets. You may have to force yourself to relate to others in a more balanced fashion.

Don't get discouraged because you can't change your life overnight. Think about your day. Think about what you can do to make your day even the slightest bit better. Perhaps it's getting fifteen more minutes of exercise, perhaps it's getting fifteen more minutes of sleep. Perhaps it's having a ten-minute conversation with your partner every morning. Perhaps it's finding a way to change your commuting schedule. Perhaps it's finding someone who can watch your children for twenty minutes, or perhaps it's finding a way to spend twenty more minutes with your children. Perhaps it's finding twenty free minutes every day to read a trashy novel, or listen to good music.

Implement that change and live with it for a week or two. Then think about another small change. Keep in mind that you can find balance by making small adjustments. The same can be true of your life; it is all spelled out in degrees. Spending an extra couple of hours every weekend doing something enjoyable with your spouse can alter the quality of your relationship. Spending fifteen minutes a day exercising can change your body. Having fewer business lunches can cut back on the amount of time pressure you feel.

Balance affects everything including your physical well-being. Are you eating more than you should? Less? Are you sleeping as much as you should? Are you sleeping more than you should? How about TV? Do you watch too much? Is drinking or smoking controlling your life?

To help you get started, ask yourself the following questions: Do you spend more time talking about putting balance into your life than you do achieving it? What are some realistic things that you could do within the next week that would put more balance into your life? What are some realistic things that you could do within the next year that would put more balance into your life?

Success Means . . .
Enjoying the Process

We started this chapter with an important quote from Carl Rogers, and now we would like to share some of our own thoughts on the subject. People who feel they have successful lives uniformly emphasize the fact that success is a process. It would appear that when it comes to the business of living, the process is everything. Though all of us have goals, there are really no final end points. Things continue to evolve. Goals change; we change. If you can't take part in the process, if you live only for some moment in the distant future, you are cheating yourself and those who love you. So write it on your bathroom mirror, on your refrigerator door, and on the visor in your car: The process is everything. Enjoy it and appreciate it while it's happening.

Epilogue

Shaping a New Wisdom

When we meet someone for the first time, what do we notice about that person? What kinds of questions are likely to be running through our minds? Let's be honest about it, do we always react to the things that count? Do we think, Gosh, that person is impressive because he/she radiates a sense of internal peace and contentment? Probably not. We are far more likely to murmur, "Look at that fabulous jacket or those great shoes." Do we ask whether he or she is a well integrated human being, or do we wonder, What does he do? Where do they live? How much does she make?

It's interesting to note that each of us is typically quick to respond to labels and externals even if we personally don't aspire to become CEOs or covet items such as Jaguar XKEs. In truth, we have been so conditioned to talk about externals that we do so almost by habit. And the converse is also true. We are so poorly schooled in articulating our real values that we rarely, if ever, give them adequate air time.

247

Every time we do this, everytime we "ooh" and "aah" over one person's material possessions or external accomplishments and fail to notice or applaud another's internal strengths, we are contributing to a system that places too much importance on externals. Every time we feel shame or embarrassment because we haven't received the money or prestige we hoped for and fail to appreciate our own intrinsic human worth, we are contributing to the lack of balance in our own lives.

If you're going to have a balanced life, one that reflects a balanced point of view, you're going to have to develop a balanced outlook. That means you're going to have to pay at least as much attention to the values you say you cherish as you do to superficialities. So one last time, let's look at some of our core values, the things we recognize as being essential to our well-being, and let's consider how each of us can better integrate them into his or her life and in so doing achieve a more complete and balanced sense of self.

A Sense of Integrity—When we think about integrity, we think about men and women whose sense of self is so strong that they are able to be true to themselves and to what they believe in. These are people who are able to live in this world in a way that doesn't compromise their internal sense of what is important, of what is right and wrong. Are you conscious of the ways in which you are able to do this? Have you prepared yourself to deal with situations in which your integrity might be tested? Remember that your integrity is involved every time you place more emphasis on your image than you do on your sense of self.

Honesty—Do you have a working definition of honesty? How far does it stretch or bend with the circumstances? Although you may be totally honest, do you sometimes forgive dishonesty in those who have power or wealth?

A Sense of Community—There are times when each of us feels isolated from the world in which we live. When this happens, we have to ask ourselves how much we are doing to maintain our connection to the larger system that is our community. Have we tried reaching out to our neighbors and the people we work with? Have we joined organizations that share our goals? Are we contributing our time and talents to further causes that are greater than ourselves?

Spirituality—What does being spiritual mean? For some people it means being part of an ongoing dialogue with God. For others it's simply having faith in some higher power. Still others say it's trying to make a deeper connection with the best parts of one's self. For some it's as basic as trying to find and maintain one's place in the universe.

We tend to ignore our spiritual lives until we're experiencing personal crises, but this is an aspect of self that needs constant attention. A spiritual life is essential in helping us keep the various aspects of our lives in perspective. It helps us see where we fit on this planet; it helps us maintain our respect for nature, the environment, and our fellow man. Your spirit is your essence; staying in touch with it means staying in touch with who you are.

Creativity—We all have creative gifts though many of us locked them away a long time ago. Do you nurture your own creative voice, and do you value your creative efforts? Do you appreciate creativity in others?

Family, Friends, and Loved Ones—Are you a caring human being? Do you show that side of yourself to those who are closest to you. Do you take the time to listen to those around you? Do you share your thoughts and feelings with them? Do you fully appreciate all the ways in which you are a loving person? Do you work at making your personal relationships strong and fulfilling. Are you maintaining a satisfying social life?

Emotional and Physical Well-being—Right now, are you doing everything you can to safeguard your physical and mental health? Do you have a Band-Aid approach to your emotions and your body, or do you have a comprehensive, holistic, preventative approach? Are you eating properly, are you getting the rest you require, and are you spending enough time in activities that are relaxing? Is having fun enough of a priority in your life?

Kindness, Sincerity, Generosity, Fairness, Decency, Humor, Charity—It's sad that so many people, from politicians to snake-oil salesmen, have turned these into buzzwords used to mask less noble motives. That shouldn't allow us to overlook the value of these instincts in others and ourselves. It's important to be kind, decent, fair, and sincere to the people around us. It's vital to maintain our sense of humor when we look at ourselves and the world around us. It's essential to work at maintaining a generous and charitable spirit. Remember: It's not always about winning.

Wisdom—Intelligence is fixed, but wisdom is acquired as we go through life. At any point, it is easy to stop and say, "I know enough," but wisdom means always being open to the kind of information that will help us make better choices. This kind of wisdom fosters real growth and real success. It allows you to abandon superficial values and turn away from temporary solutions and compromising fixes. Wisdom gives you a grasp on reality and helps you to understand when your efforts can make a difference and when it's time to let go. You need wisdom to get a sense of the long haul and to figure out what's most important in your life.

Moving On

Change does not come quickly and change does not come easily, but change does come. If you are able to improve your life for the better—and feel better about the life you have—it will be because you worked long and hard at the process, making change in tiny, often barely perceptible, increments. Ultimately, if you work hard, the cumulative effects will indeed bring you to a much different place.

Think about it this way: If you fly from New York to California in January, when you get off the plane it's almost miraculous to experience such a profound change in environment in such a short period of time. To those who are not yet jaded travelers, it's almost inspirational.

But if you walked this same distance, the experience would be an entirely different one. During that arduous trip, you would have felt exhaustion, frustration, doubt, anticipation, as well as hope. You would have experienced the differences in topography and climate. Throughout the journey, you would truly feel the distance; in the depth of your soul and on the bottoms of your feet you would know exactly how great a distance it is between New York and California.

If you want to change your life, you have to realize that you are embarking on a walking journey that will sometimes slow down to a crawl. There are no 747s to whisk you through the process, and you have to be prepared to meet many roadblocks and a wide variety of complications. There will be times when you are frightened or discouraged because everything isn't happening fast enough or isn't feeling good enough. You may discover that the people in your life are going in different directions, or that they may be slowing you down. Realistic responsibilities and obligations may force you to take some unexpected side trips. But that doesn't mean that you can't get where you want to go. If you don't get discouraged and keep moving forward, one day you will realize that you have changed for the better, and your life will have changed accordingly.

ABOUT THE AUTHORS

STEVEN CARTER and JULIA SOKOL are writers who have collaborated on three previous books, including the best-selling *Men Who Can't Love*. Steven Carter lives and works in California; Julia Sokol lives and works in Pennsylvania and New York.